Democracy in the Asia-Pacific Region

RAFIQ DOSSANI, EUGENIU HAN, CORTEZ A. COOPER III, SALE LILLY

Sponsored by the Taipei Economic and Cultural Office in Los Angeles

NATIONAL SECURITY RESEARCH DIVISION

For more information on this publication, visit **www.rand.org/t/RRA1515-1**.

About RAND

The RAND Corporation is a research organization that develops solutions to public policy challenges to help make communities throughout the world safer and more secure, healthier and more prosperous. RAND is nonprofit, nonpartisan, and committed to the public interest. To learn more about RAND, visit www.rand.org.

Research Integrity

Our mission to help improve policy and decisionmaking through research and analysis is enabled through our core values of quality and objectivity and our unwavering commitment to the highest level of integrity and ethical behavior. To help ensure our research and analysis are rigorous, objective, and nonpartisan, we subject our research publications to a robust and exacting quality-assurance process; avoid both the appearance and reality of financial and other conflicts of interest through staff training, project screening, and a policy of mandatory disclosure; and pursue transparency in our research engagements through our commitment to the open publication of our research findings and recommendations, disclosure of the source of funding of published research, and policies to ensure intellectual independence. For more information, visit www.rand.org/about/principles.

RAND's publications do not necessarily reflect the opinions of its research clients and sponsors.

Published by the RAND Corporation, Santa Monica, Calif.
© 2021 RAND Corporation
RAND® is a registered trademark.

Library of Congress Cataloging-in-Publication Data is available for this publication.
ISBN: 978-1-9774-0806-8

Cover image: Oliver Kufner_ GettyImages_and_ Dzmitry_Adobe

Limited Print and Electronic Distribution Rights

About This Report

In this report, we study democratization and the factors that influence it among small states in Asia, identify the policies that can support democratization, and examine the role that external actors can play in support of democratization. Our objective is to understand why some Asian states consolidate democratic gains while others slide toward authoritarianism, as well as the implications for policies to support democratic consolidation. We follow a three-stage approach: (1) a literature review to identify global and Asian trends in democratization and to identify influential factors from the economic, social, political, and geopolitical domains; (2) a statistical analysis to discover significant democratization factors for Asia relative to global democratization factors; and (3) interview-based case studies of four Asian states—Taiwan, Thailand, Sri Lanka, and Malaysia—at different stages of democratization. The study was conducted in 2020 and 2021. This research will be of value to policymakers who are interested in the subject of strengthening Asia's democratization.

RAND National Security Research Division

This research was sponsored by the Taipei Economic and Cultural Office in Los Angeles and conducted within the International Security and Defense Policy Center of the RAND National Security Research Division (NSRD). NSRD conducts research and analysis for the Office of the Secretary of Defense, the U.S. Intelligence Community, the U.S. State Department, allied foreign governments, and foundations.

For more information on the RAND International Security and Defense Policy Center, see www.rand.org/nsrd/isdp or contact the director (contact information is provided on the webpage).

Acknowledgments

The authors acknowledge the support of the Taipei Economic and Cultural Office in Los Angeles. We would like to thank all of the interviewees, who gave generously of their time and knowledge to convey their understanding of this difficult topic. Finally, we thank the reviewers of this report, Angela O'Mahony and Shiv Shankar Menon, for their time, expertise, and diligence.

Summary

In this report, we study democratization and the factors that influence it among small states in Asia, identify the policies that can support democratization, and examine the role that external actors can play in support of democratization.

Our study approach has three parts: (1) a literature review to identify global and Asian trends in democratization and to identify influential factors from the economic, social, political, and geopolitical domains; (2) a statistical analysis to discover significant democratization factors for Asia relative to global democratization factors; and (3) interview-based case studies of four Asian states at different stages of democratization. These states are classified by the Regimes of the World index as a liberal democracy (Taiwan), a closed autocracy (Thailand), an electoral democracy (Sri Lanka), and an electoral autocracy (Malaysia). We use the case studies to examine the relevance of the factors that result from our statistical analysis and to discover determinants that are specific to the countries studied. Our findings are as follows:

- From our literature review and analysis of secondary data, we found that, globally and in Asia, there has been a reduction in the number of autocracies over time and, offsetting this, a rise in the number of partial democracies. The latter trend is due to both the retention of some autocratic institutions among new democracies and backsliding among previously liberal democracies.
- We explored modernization theory as a driver of democratization, leading to the identification of four classes of factors for further study: socioeconomic, political and governance, international linkages, and civil society participation.
- Our statistical modeling showed that several factors that are significantly associated with democratization globally also apply to Asia. These are the gross domestic product (GDP) per capita, human capital, and urbanization (socioeconomic factors); civil society participation and women's political empowerment (civil society factors); and independence of the judiciary, independence of subfederal units, and corruption (political and governance factors). Surprisingly, inequality, voter turnout, and quality of government, although significantly associated with democratization in our global analysis, are not significantly associated with democratization in Asia. External alliances (international linkages) are significant for Asia but are not globally significant. The GDP growth rate and trade openness are insignificant both globally and for Asia.
- Our country case studies showed that transitions to conditions of both greater democracy and less democracy can occur without disruption to a country's normal political process. Malaysia and Sri Lanka provide examples of such transitions.
- Democratization (both democratic consolidation and transitions to democracy) can face significant hurdles. Economic growth can be used to legitimize authoritarian rule, as in the cases of Malaysia and Thailand. Ethnic diversity, a hallmark of the typical Asian state, can hurt democratization, as in the cases of Malaysia and Sri Lanka. Malaysian politicians from the ethnic majority community created stable, communally based ruling coalitions with ethnic minority communities, crowding out secular parties. In Sri Lanka, suppression of the Tamil insurgency was accompanied by the rise of majoritarian governance.
- Voter participation does not correlate well with democratization in Asia. Voter participation in Asia tends to be high regardless of the state of democracy. Taiwan's and Malaysia's rates of voter participation regularly average over 70 percent. Thailand's voter turnout rate has been more volatile but still averages over 60 percent, as does Sri Lanka's.

- Media freedom is closely related to the state of democracy. For instance, the Malaysian media was tightly controlled during the country's authoritarian period and has become freer, with greater democracy, in recent years. Thailand's media has become less free in recent years with the shift to autocracy. Sri Lanka's media lost significant freedom during the country's period of autocracy but regained its freedom once the autocratic period ended.
- Civil society organizations flourish during periods of democratization, but their depth and resilience do not seem to be related to the state of democracy. This has been the case for Malaysia, Sri Lanka, and Taiwan.
- The judiciary is invariably an important player, but its role can both hurt democratization and help it.
- External actors are usually marginal players in a country's democratization and are more effective when their role is noncoercive, which is consistent with our statistical analysis. Membership in regional and international institutions has not helped with democratization. The presence of a large, influence-seeking regional or global player (primarily the United States and China in Asia, India in South Asia) does not seem to have affected democratization. The possible exception, although indirect, is Taiwan.

The policy recommendations arising from our study are as follows:

- The governments of fragile democracies should, during democratic upturns, seek to embed into law and practice the features that promote democratization. These include regular elections, investment in human capital, legal changes to empower women and strengthen the independence of civil society, the independence of the judiciary and subfederal units, the freedom of the media, and the tackling of corruption.
- During democratic downturns, civil society should use grassroots movements and legal activism to ensure that as many pro-democracy features as were in practice during the prior democratic period are protected.
- Sympathetic external actors that are full democracies should prioritize the "soft" areas mentioned above—such as promoting women's empowerment—rather than offer defense and diplomatic support if they wish to help other countries democratize.

Contents

Figures and Tables

Figures

Tables

CHAPTER ONE

Introduction

In this report, we study trends in democratization among small states in Asia and the factors that influence these trends.[1] We address the following questions: Why do some Asian states consolidate democratic gains while others slide toward authoritarianism? What policies can support democratic consolidation? Can external actors help?

The report proceeds as follows. In Chapter Two, we conduct a literature review to identify global and Asian trends in democratization and to identify influential factors from the economic, social, political, and geopolitical domains, focusing on the postcolonial period (1951 onward).

Next, in Chapter Three, we undertake a statistical analysis to discover factors identified from the literature review that might be significantly associated with democratization in Asia. We also undertake a similar analysis using global data in order to identify factors that might be significantly associated with democratization globally. A comparison of the significant factors for Asia and the world shows that, although there are several globally significant factors that are also significant for Asia, some globally significant factors are not significant for Asia and some factors that are significant for Asia are not significant globally.

Recognizing that there could be unique factors, such as ethnic composition and location, that might not be captured by our statistical analysis, in Chapter Four, we examine four Asian states that are at different stages of democratization: a liberal democracy (Taiwan), a closed autocracy (Thailand), an electoral autocracy (Malaysia), and an electoral democracy (Sri Lanka).[2] Our case studies show the existence of variations in the influence of different factors in different countries. This helps explain the findings of the statistical analysis.

Finally, in Chapter Five, we consolidate the findings of the case studies to identify factors that could be instruments of policy and to develop policy recommendations.

---

[1] In this study, *Asia* includes East Asia, South Asia, and Southeast Asia. We exclude Central Asia and West Asia.

[2] Stages of democratization are from the Regimes of the World index published in the Varieties of Democracy (V-Dem) data sets. See Anna Lührmann, Marcus Tannenberg, and Staffan I. Lindberg, "Regimes of the World (RoW): Opening New Avenues for the Comparative Study of Political Regimes," *Politics and Governance*, Vol. 6, No. 1, 2018.

CHAPTER TWO

Literature Review

Dahl defines *democracy* as a political system that has the quality of being "completely or almost completely responsive to its citizens."[1] Dahl and Shapiro list six required political institutions: elected officials; free, fair, and frequent elections; freedom of expression; alternative sources of information; associational autonomy; and inclusive citizenship.[2] Przeworski opts for a more minimalist definition of democracy, as a "political arrangement in which people select government through elections and have a reasonable possibility of removing incumbent governments they do not like."[3]

In this report, we adopt the Polity Project's definition of democracy as a political system that is based on free and fair elections, the rule of law, and individual freedoms.[4] To measure it, we rely primarily on a set of standardized democracy measures developed by the V-Dem Institute,[5] the Polity Project,[6] Freedom House,[7] and the Economist Intelligence Unit.[8]

The worldwide evolution of democracy since 1951 has been uneven. The list of states that have flipped from autocracy to democracy has grown—sometimes steadily, sometimes in waves—because of key events both external and internal to the democratizing countries. In 2002, democracies surpassed autocracies in number for the first time, only for this trend to be reversed in 2019 (Figure 2.1).

Although the number of *closed autocracies*—countries with no multiparty elections for the chief executive or the legislature—has generally been falling over the past seven decades, the number of *partial democracies*, including electoral democracies and electoral autocracies, has been rising (Figure 2.2). This trend has

---

[1]   Robert A. Dahl, *Polyarchy: Participation and Opposition*, New Haven, Conn.: Yale University Press, 1971, p. 2.

[2]   Robert A. Dahl and Ian Shapiro, *On Democracy*, 2nd ed., New Haven, Conn.: Yale University Press, 2015, Ch. 8.

[3]   Adam Przeworski, *Crises of Democracy*, Cambridge, United Kingdom: Cambridge University Press, 2019, p. 5.

[4]   Monty G. Marshall and Ted Robert Gurr, *Polity 5: Political Regime Characteristics and Transitions, 1800–2018: Dataset Users' Manual*, Vienna, Va.: Center for Systemic Peace, April 23, 2020.

[5]   Michael Coppedge, John Gerring, Carl Henrik Knutsen, Staffan I. Lindberg, Jan Teorell, David Altman, Michael Bernhard, M. Steven Fish, Adam Glynn, Allen Hicken, et al., *V-Dem Codebook*, version 10, Gothenburg, Sweden: University of Gothenburg, Varieties of Democracy Institute, Varieties of Democracy Project, March 2020. V-Dem classifies countries into four possible regimes: closed autocracy, electoral autocracy, electoral democracy, and liberal democracy. An *electoral democracy* satisfies the requirements of de facto free and fair multiparty elections and a minimum number of Dahl's institutional prerequisites but does not satisfy access to justice; transparent law enforcement; or liberal principles of respect for personal liberties, rule of law, and judicial and legislative constraints on the executive. An *electoral autocracy* is characterized by de jure multiparty elections for the chief executive and the legislature but a failure to achieve elections that are free and fair, de facto multiparty elections, or a minimum number of Dahl's institutional prerequisites of polyarchy.

[6]   Marshall and Gurr, 2020.

[7]   Freedom House, "Countries and Territories," webpage, undated.

[8]   Economist Intelligence Unit, *Democracy Index 2020: In Sickness and in Health?* London, 2021. Most democracy measures are highly correlated over time (Jan Teorell, Michael Coppedge, Svend-Erik Skaaning, and Staffan I. Lindberg, "Measuring Electoral Democracy with V-Dem Data: Introducing a New Polyarchy Index," Gothenburg, Sweden: Varieties of Democracy Institute, Working Paper 25, March 2016).

FIGURE 2.1

Democracies and Autocracies Since 1900

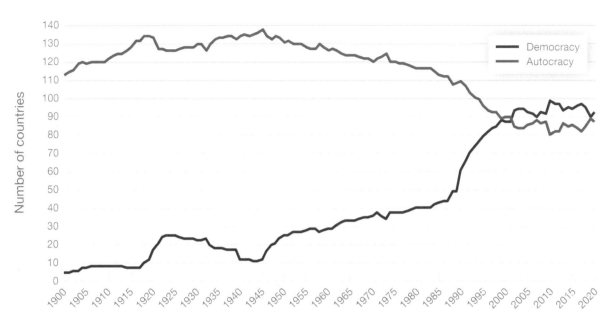

SOURCE: Created with data from Michael Coppedge, John Gerring, Carl Henrik Knutsen, Staffan I. Lindberg, Jan Teorell, David Altman, Michael Bernhard, Agnes Cornell, M. Steven Fish, Lisa Gastaldi, et al., *V-Dem Codebook*, version 11.1, Gothenburg, Sweden: University of Gothenburg, Varieties of Democracy Institute, Varieties of Democracy Project, March 2021.

NOTE: Democracies = the sum of electoral democracies and liberal democracies. Autocracies = the sum of closed autocracies and electoral autocracies.

FIGURE 2.2

Evolution of Political Regimes Since 1900

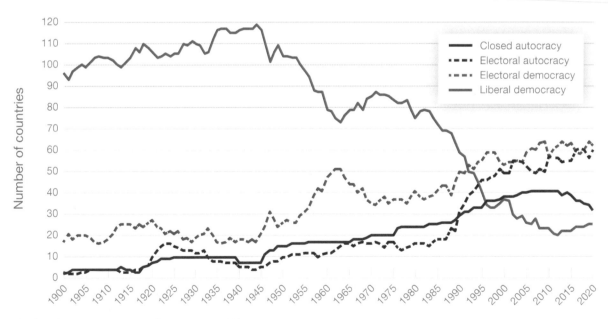

SOURCE: Created with data from Coppedge et al., 2021.

been partly due to the retention of some autocratic institutions among new democracies as well as backsliding among previously liberal democracies. Not counted in the democratic advance are countries that have adopted the veneer of democratic institutions by having multiparty elections for the chief executive and the legislature, but not the type of elections that can be considered free and fair. These countries are classified as *electoral autocracies.*

At the same time that trends among "flawed" democracies have worsened,[9] the number of *full* (also termed *liberal*) democracies has been flat for the past two decades. Some analysts have argued that democratization has stalled or, even worse, is in retreat. The "third wave of autocratization" is mostly affecting those democracies that experience gradual setbacks that are hidden under a "legal façade."[10] The number of full democracies in 2019 was the lowest since the inception of the Economist Intelligence Unit index in 2006.[11]

Between 2015 and 2019, liberal democracy scores declined in all regions except the Asia Pacific. In fact, the Asia Pacific has been the only region for which decadal democracy scores have improved over the past two decades.[12] Figure 2.3 shows democratization trends in the past 50 years. The solid black line is the average score of the *liberal democracy* variable in the Asia-Pacific region, and the gray shading represents the confidence interval.[13]

FIGURE 2.3
The Evolution of Electoral Democracy by Region

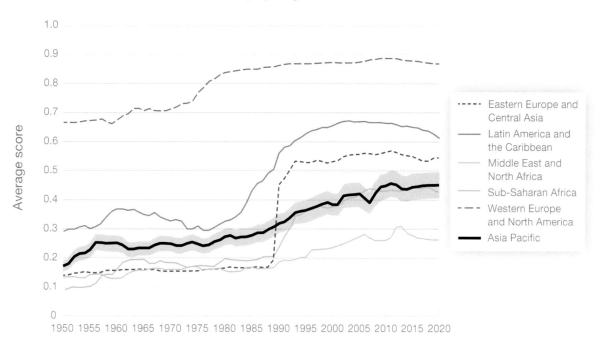

SOURCE: Created using data from the electoral democracy index in Coppedge et al., 2021.

---

[9] Economist Intelligence Unit, *Democracy Index 2019: A Year of Democratic Setbacks and Popular Protest*, London, 2020.

[10] The "first wave of autocratization" occurred between the late 1920s and the late 1930s, and the "second wave" occurred between the early 1960s and the mid-1970s (Anna Lührmann and Staffan I. Lindberg, "A Third Wave of Autocratization Is Here: What Is New About It?" *Democratization*, Vol. 26, No. 7, 2019).

[11] Economist Intelligence Unit, 2020.

[12] The liberal democracy scores are averages by region in which all countries within a region are weighted equally.

[13] The confidence interval reflects one standard deviation from the mean.

Over the past decade, Myanmar, Fiji, Malaysia, Sri Lanka, the Solomon Islands, and South Korea significantly improved their average scores, while the average scores of Bangladesh, Thailand, Pakistan, the Philippines, and India declined (Figure 2.4). Notably, Myanmar, Fiji, and Sri Lanka showed improvements across the board, while India, Bangladesh, and Thailand witnessed significant decreases in most indexes (Table 2.1). However, as shown by the illiberal trend in India since 2014 and the coup in Myanmar in February 2021, the stability of democracy is questionable in both long-established and recently established democracies.

Theories of Democratization

Democratization can refer to several processes: the transition from a nondemocratic regime to a democratic regime, the deepening of democracy in a state that is already democratic, and the survival of democratic regimes.[14]

Some scholars argue that the preference for democracy is natural in all societies. For example, Acemoglu and Robinson maintain that the masses will always have "a stronger preference for democracy than elites"[15] because every society has contests over the distribution of resources, and democracies tend to better manage mass interests than do autocracies. However, this assertion ignores the complex nature of the choices that

FIGURE 2.4
Democratization Trends in Select Asian Countries

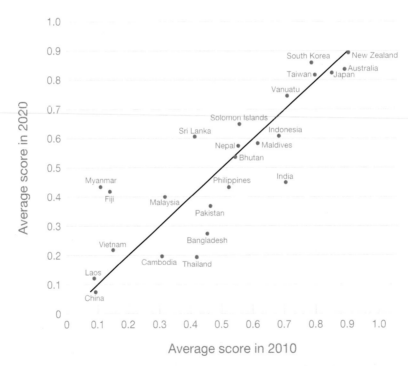

SOURCE: Created using data from the electoral democracy index in Coppedge et al., 2021.
NOTE: Countries above the solid black line improved their scores in 2020 relative to 2010.

---

[14] Christian Welzel, "Theories of Democratization," in Christian Haerpfer, Patrick Bernhagen, Christian Welzel, and Ronald F. Inglehart, eds., *Democratization*, 2nd ed., Oxford, United Kingdom: Oxford University Press, 2019.

[15] Daron Acemoglu and James A. Robinson, *Economic Origins of Dictatorship and Democracy*, New York: Cambridge University Press, 2006, p. 22.

TABLE 2.1
Democratization in Select Asian Countries (2009–2019)

Country/Region	Clean Elections Index	Freedom of Association	Freedom of Expression	Equality Before the Law and Individual Liberty Index	Judicial Constraints on the Executive	Legislative Constraints on the Executive	Egalitarian Component Index	Participatory Component Index	Deliberative Component Index	Polarization of Society
Taiwan	Improved	Unchanged	Deteriorated	Deteriorated	Improved	Improved	Improved	Deteriorated	Improved	Deteriorated
South Korea	Improved	Unchanged	Improved	Improved	Improved	Improved	Deteriorated	Improved	Improved	Improved
Japan	Improved	Unchanged	Deteriorated	Deteriorated	Deteriorated	Improved	Deteriorated	Deteriorated	Deteriorated	Deteriorated
India	Deteriorated	Unchanged	Deteriorated	Deteriorated	Deteriorated	Deteriorated	Deteriorated	Deteriorated	Deteriorated	Deteriorated
Bhutan	Improved	Unchanged	Deteriorated	Improved	Improved	Improved	Unchanged	Improved	Improved	Deteriorated
Pakistan	Deteriorated	Unchanged	Deteriorated	Deteriorated	Deteriorated	Improved	Deteriorated	Deteriorated	Improved	Deteriorated
Bangladesh	Deteriorated	Unchanged	Deteriorated	Deteriorated	Deteriorated	Deteriorated	Deteriorated	Deteriorated	Deteriorated	Deteriorated
Burma/Myanmar	Improved	Improved	Improved	Improved	Improved	Improved	Improved	Improved	Improved	Improved
Sri Lanka	Improved	Unchanged	Improved	Improved	Improved	Improved	Improved	Improved	Improved	Improved
Maldives	Deteriorated	Unchanged	Deteriorated	Improved	Improved	Deteriorated	Deteriorated	Deteriorated	Improved	Deteriorated
Nepal	Improved	Unchanged	Deteriorated	Deteriorated	Deteriorated	Deteriorated	Deteriorated	Improved	Deteriorated	Deteriorated
Thailand	Deteriorated	Deteriorated	Deteriorated	Deteriorated	Deteriorated	Deteriorated	Deteriorated	Deteriorated	Deteriorated	Improved
Cambodia	Deteriorated	Deteriorated	Deteriorated	Deteriorated	Improved	Deteriorated	Deteriorated	Deteriorated	Deteriorated	Deteriorated
Laos	Improved	Unchanged	Improved	Improved	Deteriorated	Improved	Improved	Improved	Improved	Deteriorated
Vietnam	Improved	Unchanged	Deteriorated	Deteriorated	Deteriorated	Improved	Deteriorated	Deteriorated	Deteriorated	Deteriorated
Malaysia	Improved	Unchanged	Improved	Improved	Improved	Improved	Improved	Deteriorated	Improved	Deteriorated
Singapore	Deteriorated	Unchanged	Improved	Improved	Deteriorated	Improved	Improved	Deteriorated	Improved	Deteriorated
Philippines	Improved	Unchanged	Deteriorated	Deteriorated	Deteriorated	Deteriorated	Deteriorated	Deteriorated	Deteriorated	Deteriorated
Indonesia	Deteriorated	Unchanged	Deteriorated	Improved	Deteriorated	Improved	Deteriorated	Improved	Deteriorated	Deteriorated
Timor-Leste	Improved	Unchanged	Improved	Deteriorated	Deteriorated	Improved	Improved	Improved	Improved	Deteriorated
Papua New Guinea	Deteriorated	Unchanged	Improved	Deteriorated	Deteriorated	Deteriorated	Deteriorated	Unchanged	Deteriorated	Improved
Vanuatu	Improved	Unchanged	Deteriorated	Deteriorated	Improved	Improved	Deteriorated	Improved	Improved	Improved
Solomon Islands	Improved	Unchanged	Improved	Improved	Improved	Improved	Improved	Improved	Deteriorated	Unchanged
Fiji	Improved	Improved	Improved	Improved	Improved	Improved	Improved	Improved	Improved	Improved

SOURCE: Created using data from Coppedge et al., 2020.

the electorate faces in a typical election, and resource reallocation might not be a dominant interest of the masses.

Prior to World War II, emerging class struggles in Europe sometimes gave birth to authoritarian regimes, such as fascism and communism.[16] In developing countries, different factors were at work.[17] In the post-colonial period, population growth, industrialization, and the associated rise of the working class were never sufficient for the formation of stable, mature democracies because the postcolonial states had to contend with a complex mix of the colonial experience, social churn, nationalism, World War II, and modernization.[18]

Once a democratic transition has been achieved, the focus of democratization tends to shift to the *consolidation* of democracy, which can be broadly defined as the process of securing the new democracy by extending its life expectancy and preventing backsliding to authoritarianism.[19] Democratic consolidation includes various aspects of the diffusion of democratic values, the protection of civil liberties, civilian control of the military, party-building, electoral rules, decentralization, judicial reforms, and myriad other aspects of the political system and society more broadly.

Modernization Theory and Its Factors

In this section, we identify factors that contribute to democratic transition and consolidation. Underlying these factors is the role of modernization as a driver of democratization. Inglehart and Welzel note, "The core concept of modernization theory is that economic development produces systematic changes in society and politics."[20] Although this does not necessarily imply that the systematic changes promote democratization, as pointed out by these authors, the empirical reality of an overall positive relationship between economic development and democracy has led researchers to argue that there are systematic factors that are necessary for democracy to develop, even if they are not sufficient, and to look for the systematic changes that influence democratization.[21]

Socioeconomic factors are central to modernization theory. The key factors identified in this category are education,[22] economic growth,[23] and urbanization.[24] These factors are interrelated; for instance, the relation-

---

[16] Acemoglu and Robinson, 2006.

[17] The authors are grateful to one of the reviewers for this insight.

[18] Andreas Schedler, "What Is Democratic Consolidation?" *Journal of Democracy*, Vol. 9, No. 2, April 1998.

[19] Schedler, 1998.

[20] Ronald Inglehart and Christian Welzel, "Changing Mass Priorities: The Link Between Modernization and Democracy," *Perspectives on Politics*, Vol. 8, No. 2, June 2010, p. 553.

[21] Seymour Martin Lipset, "Some Social Requisites of Democracy: Economic Development and Political Legitimacy," *American Political Science Review*, Vol. 53, No. 1, March 1959. For an insightful overview of modernization theory, see Daniel Treisman, "Triggering Democracy," *Annals of Comparative Democratization*, Vol. 16, No. 3, September 2018.

[22] Gabriel Abraham Almond and Sidney Verba, *The Civic Culture: Political Attitudes and Democracy in Five Nations*, Princeton, N.J.: Princeton University Press, 2015.

[23] James S. Coleman, "Conclusion: The Political Systems of the Developing Areas," in Gabriel Abraham Almond and James Smoot Coleman, eds., *The Politics of the Developing Areas*, Princeton, N.J.: Princeton University Press, 1960; and Lipset, 1959.

[24] Almond and Verba, 2015; Coleman, 2015; Daniel Lerner, *The Passing of Traditional Society: Modernizing the Middle East*, Glencoe, Ill.: Free Press, 1958; and Lipset, 1959.

ship between urbanization and education has been noted in the literature,[25] as has the relationship between education and economic growth.[26]

A large middle class and limited economic inequality, which arise from urbanization, with its attendant implications for industrialization and an educated workforce, as argued by Lerner,[27] are also seen in global studies as positive influences on democratic power transfers between different groups and, thus, important for democratic sustainability.[28]

Modernization theory would suggest that, as the world's most economically dynamic continent, Asia should be largely democratic. However, the typical Asian state has not democratized at the same pace that its economy has developed. In East Asia, with the exception of postwar Japan, developmentally minded dictators initially promoted the successful East Asian model of development. Later transitions to democracy occurred in Korea and Taiwan via carefully engineered institutions that favored effectiveness and accountability over representativeness to preserve elevated growth rates. By contrast, Southeast Asia remains largely undemocratic while successfully pursuing the same East Asian model of development. South Asia, another contrast, has seen significant democratic backsliding in the present century despite, as predicted in global studies, its socioeconomic progress, albeit at a more moderate pace than the rest of Asia.[29]

The diversity of Asian states' experiences might arise from these states' different stages of development. Kanbur and Zhuang's 2013 study of the effect of urbanization on inequality in four Asian countries (China, India, Indonesia, and the Philippines) shows that, in countries in the study's sample with low urbanization rates (India and Indonesia), rising urbanization exacerbated inequality, while the reverse was true in the countries with high urbanization rates (China and the Philippines).[30]

Modernization via urbanization is also associated with an increase in the capacity and role of civil society in democratization.[31] Haggard and Kaufman show that grassroots civil society activism, such as labor unions, can be a potent force for democratization in lower- and middle-income countries.[32]

Alagappa looks at the development of civil society in Asia and finds that civil society organizations played prominent roles in advocating for political liberalization in South Korea, Taiwan, the Philippines, Thailand, and Indonesia.[33] At the same time, Alagappa concludes that "there is no necessary connection between the rise of civil society and democratic change."[34] Civil society may support democracy when it is rooted in dem-

---

[25] Roland Andersson, John M. Quigley, and Mats Wilhelmsson, "Urbanization, Productivity, and Innovation: Evidence from Investment in Higher Education," *Journal of Urban Economics*, Vol. 66, No. 1, July 2009.

[26] Eric A. Hanushek and Ludger Woessmann, "Education and Economic Growth," *Economics of Education*, 2010.

[27] Lerner, 1958.

[28] Torben Iversen and David Soskice, *Democracy and Prosperity: Reinventing Capitalism Through a Turbulent Century*, Princeton, N.J.: Princeton University Press, 2019; and Tatu Vanhanen, *Democratization: A Comparative Analysis of 170 Countries*, London: Routledge, 2004.

[29] Adam Przeworski, Michael E. Alvarez, José Antonio Cheibub, and Fernando Limongi, *Democracy and Development: Political Institutions and Well-Being in the World, 1950–1990*, Cambridge, United Kingdom: Cambridge University Press, 2000.

[30] Ravi Kanbur and Juzhong Zhuang, "Urbanization and Inequality in Asia," *Asian Development Review*, Vol. 30, No. 1, 2013.

[31] Claire Mercer, "NGOs, Civil Society and Democratization: A Critical Review of the Literature," *Progress in Development Studies*, Vol. 2, No. 1, January 1, 2002.

[32] Stephan Haggard and Robert R. Kaufman, *Dictators and Democrats: Masses, Elites, and Regime Change*, Princeton, N.J.: Princeton University Press, 2016a; and Stephan Haggard and Robert R. Kaufman, "Democratization During the Third Wave," *Annual Review of Political Science*, Vol. 19, May 2016b.

[33] Muthiah Alagappa, ed., *Civil Society and Political Change in Asia: Expanding and Contracting Democratic Space*, Stanford: Stanford University Press, 2004.

[34] Alagappa, 2004, p. 479.

ocratic ideals and not dominated by organizations with totalizing goals, and, even under the right conditions, civil society is a necessary but not sufficient condition for democratic development.[35]

Women's empowerment is an important and understudied factor in the evolution of civil society and democratization. Waylen's 1994 review of the literature on women and democratization and evidence from Europe and Latin America found that, in Latin America, "Women's mobilization . . . was clearly very important in bringing about the initial breakdown and opening . . . . [W]omen's protests formed the first organized and open opposition to authoritarian governments."[36] Huang noted that, despite Asia having many female government leaders, women's political participation in Asia is lower than in Europe, the Americas, and Africa, a phenomenon that is evident even in liberal democracies, such as Japan and South Korea.[37]

Acemoglu and Robinson argue that fixed national effects—composed of a nation's institutional, political, and cultural heritage—matter more than economic development.[38] Inglehart and Welzel suggest, in the same vein, that cultural values are key systematic values that can promote democratization, particularly the diminution of a traditional values dimension in favor of secular, rational values and a similar decline of survival values relative to self-expression values.[39]

By contrast, Arat, while noting the importance of societal changes, argues for developing a structural basis to understand the societal changes.[40] Arat focuses on understanding how political and governance factors matter and finds that political participation, party competitiveness, and civil liberties influence democratic transition. Przeworski sees democracy as a "mechanism for processing conflicts" in liberty and civil peace, thus allowing the political forces to "temporarily tolerate unfavorable outcomes."[41] Bermeo's 2016 analysis of democratic backsliding notes that open-ended coups d'état, executive coups, and election-day vote fraud have significantly diminished over time, while promissory coups, executive aggrandizement, and strategic harassment and manipulation are unchanged or on the rise.[42] Notably, the person or group who is undertaking any of these three types of democratic breakdown—promissory coups, executive aggrandizement, or strategic harassment and manipulation—often claims that their action is intended to defend democracy.

In this century, free trade has been an important driver of economic growth. López-Córdova and Meissner argue for the importance of trade for democratization.[43] Democratization can happen when a trade agreement constrains governments to maintain free markets at home, reduces economic rents that authori-

---

[35] Alagappa, 2004, pp. 479–480.

[36] Georgina Waylen, "Women and Democratization: Conceptualizing Gender Relations in Transition Politics," *World Politics*, Vol. 46, No. 3, April 1994, p. 339.

[37] In Asia, women's leadership in politics has almost always been limited to women from politically powerful families, such as Sirimavo Bandaranaike of Sri Lanka, Indira Gandhi of India, Benazir Bhutto of Pakistan, Gloria Macapagal Arroyo of the Philippines, Sheikh Hasina of Bangladesh, Megawati Sukarnoputri of Indonesia, Aung San Suu Kyi of Myanmar, and Tsai Ing-wen of Taiwan (Chang-Ling Huang, "Women's Political Empowerment," in Tun-jen Cheng and Yun-han Chu, eds., *Routledge Handbook of Democratization in East Asia*, London: Routledge, 2017).

[38] Acemoglu and Robinson, 2006.

[39] Inglehart and Welzel, 2010.

[40] Zehra F. Arat, "Democracy and Economic Development: Modernization Theory Revisited," *Comparative Politics*, Vol. 21, No. 1, October 1988.

[41] Przeworski, 2019, p. 150.

[42] Nancy Bermeo, "On Democratic Backsliding," *Journal of Democracy*, Vol. 27, No. 1, January 2016.

[43] J. Ernesto López-Córdova and Christopher M. Meissner, "The Impact of International Trade on Democracy: A Long-Run Perspective," *World Politics*, Vol. 60, No. 4, July 2008.

tarians may rely on, or even explicitly promotes democracy.[44] However, the effect of increased international linkages is not always positive. Increased trade may lead to higher domestic inequality and workers' displacement, which in turn may lead to domestic polarization and increased popular support for nativist or extreme political forces, as recent U.S. and European experiences show.[45]

Asian countries seem to be different from countries in other world regions in terms of their reaction to globalization, perhaps because Asia has had a more positive experience than the rest of the world has had. For instance, Taniguchi found that the growth in imports from China positively affected manufacturing employment in Japan.[46] As a result, Asian countries have been at the forefront of globalization and are typically strong promoters of international economic relations, as Figure 2.5 shows.

Another type of international linkage that could affect democratization is a country's diplomatic and military alliances and partnerships. Lai and Reiter argue that international alliances or other strategic part-

FIGURE 2.5
Participation in Regional Trade Agreements

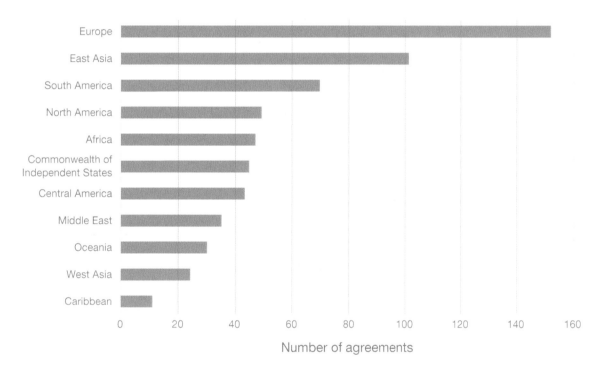

SOURCE: World Trade Organization, "Regional Trade Agreements," database, undated.

---

[44] Xuepeng Liu and Emanuel Ornelas, "Free Trade Agreements and the Consolidation of Democracy," *American Economic Journal: Macroeconomics*, Vol. 6, No. 2, 2014; and Jon C. Pevehouse, "Democracy from the Outside-In? International Organizations and Democratization," *International Organization*, Vol. 56, No. 3, Summer 2002, p. 522.

[45] David Autor, David Dorn, Gordon Hanson, and Kaveh Majlesi, "Importing Political Polarization? The Electoral Consequences of Rising Trade Exposure," *American Economic Review*, Vol. 110, No. 10, 2020; and Italo Colantone and Piero Stanig, "The Trade Origins of Economic Nationalism: Import Competition and Voting Behavior in Western Europe," *American Journal of Political Science*, Vol. 62, No. 4, October 2018.

[46] Mina Taniguchi, "The Effect of an Increase in Imports from China on Local Labor Markets in Japan," *Journal of the Japanese and International Economies*, Vol. 51, March 2019.

nerships are more likely between regimes of the same type than between regimes of dissimilar types.[47] This finding seems to be particularly relevant for Asian states, which have a long postcolonial record of alliances and partnerships with great powers within and outside Asia—some democratic, some authoritarian—that have a record of influencing domestic politics in their partner countries.

Asian experience shows that regional arrangements may strengthen the domestic coalitions that advocate for a country's membership in the regional arrangement, although this does not necessarily strengthen democratization. Asian regional agreements, such as the Association of Southeast Asian Nations (ASEAN) and the South Asian Association for Regional Cooperation, have historically not promoted democracy through defense or diplomatic arrangements. The Shanghai Cooperation Organisation is another example of an Asian regional arrangement that has not promoted democracy.

A summary of findings from the literature is presented in Appendix A. Drawing from these insights, in the next chapter, we consider socioeconomic factors, institutional and political factors, civil society factors, and international linkages in our analysis of Asian countries.

---

[47] Brian Lai and Dan Reiter, "Democracy, Political Similarity, and International Alliances, 1816–1992," *Journal of Conflict Resolution*, Vol. 44, No. 2, April 2000.

CHAPTER THREE

Democratization in the Data

In Chapter Two, we identified factors that are significantly associated with democratization globally. Of these, the factors selected for further analysis and their corresponding indicators are listed in Table 3.1.

The data, sources, and statistical model that we used are described in detail in Appendix B. Table B.1 in Appendix B presents the descriptive statistics of the data. Here, we present the results of our analysis (Tables 3.2 and 3.3).

Our statistical analysis shows that several factors that are globally significant are also significant in Asia. These are the gross domestic product (GDP) per capita, human capital, and urbanization (socioeconomic factors); civil society participation and women's political empowerment (civil society factors); and independence of the judiciary, independence of subfederal units, and corruption (political and governance factors). Surprisingly, urbanization, inequality, voter turnout, and quality of government, although significantly associated with democratization in our global analysis, are not significantly associated with democratization in Asia. External alliances (international linkages) are significant for Asia but are not globally significant. The GDP growth rate and trade openness are insignificant factors both globally and for Asia.

In the next chapter, we examine these factors using case studies.

TABLE 3.1
Factors and Corresponding Indicators

Factor	Indicators
Economic growth	Real GDP per capita, GDP growth rate
Middle class	Urbanization, inequality (share of income of richest 1 percent of the population)
Human capital	Composite human capital index, based on years of schooling and returns to education
Systems for democratic consolidation	Independence of the judiciary, existence of independent subfederal units, corruption, voter turnout, quality of government
International linkages	Number of alliances in any given year, trade openness
Civil society	Women's political empowerment, civil society participation
Control variable	Democracy score in the previous year[a]

[a] The democracy score is one of the four measures presented in Table B.1 in Appendix B.

TABLE 3.2

Socioeconomic Factors: Pooled Ordinary Least Squares (year fixed effects)

Dependent Variable	Polity Revised Combined Score		V-Dem Polyarchy Index		Freedom House Political Rights Index		Freedom House Civil Liberties Index	
	World	Asia	World	Asia	World	Asia	World	Asia
GDP per capita	0.04	0.15	0.12*	0.41*	0.02**	0.03	0.02***	0.04*
	(0.02)	(0.09)	(0.06)	(0.19)	(0.01)	(0.03)	(0.01)	(0.02)
GDP growth rate	−0.01**	−0.03*	0.01	−0.03	−0.00	−0.01	−0.00	−0.00
	(0.00)	(0.01)	(0.01)	(0.04)	(0.00)	(0.01)	(0.00)	(0.00)
Human capital index	0.23***	0.30*	0.51***	0.90*	0.10***	0.12*	0.09***	0.13***
	(0.04)	(0.14)	(0.12)	(0.39)	(0.02)	(0.05)	(0.01)	(0.03)
Urbanization	0.00*	0.00	0.01**	0.01	0.00**	0.00	0.00***	0.00*
	(0.00)	(0.00)	(0.00)	(0.01)	(0.00)	(0.00)	(0.00)	(0.00)
Inequality (top 1 percent)	−2.35***	−3.75	−8.78***	−14.80	−1.03***	−1.41	−0.94***	−1.12
	(0.68)	(2.90)	(2.58)	(7.72)	(0.29)	(1.28)	(0.24)	(0.71)

SOURCES: Center for Systemic Peace, "The Polity Project," webpage, undated; Coppedge et al., 2020; Coppedge et al., 2021; and Freedom House, undated.
NOTES: *$p < 0.05$; **$p < 0.01$; ***$p < 0.001$. Standard errors in parentheses.

TABLE 3.3

Political and Governance, Civil Society, and International Linkages Factors: Pooled Ordinary Least Squares (year fixed effects)

Dependent Variable	Polity Revised Combined Score		V-Dem Polyarchy Index		Freedom House Political Rights Index		Freedom House Civil Liberties Index	
	World	Asia	World	Asia	World	Asia	World	Asia
Voter turnout	0.00	0.00	0.02***	0.03	0.00	−0.00	0.00***	0.00
	(0.00)	(0.00)	(0.00)	(0.01)	(0.00)	(0.00)	(0.00)	(0.00)
Independent judiciary	0.16**	0.31	0.84***	1.09	0.12***	0.18*	0.11***	0.13**
	(0.06	(0.20	(0.22)	(0.72)	(0.02)	(0.08)	(0.02)	(0.04)
Independent subfederal unit	0.09	−0.21	0.18	−1.00***	0.04*	−0.10*	0.04*	−0.04
	(0.06)	(0.14)	(0.16)	(0.26)	(0.02)	(0.04)	(0.02)	(0.03)
Women's political empowerment	0.85***	1.14**	3.42***	2.76**	0.51***	0.39*	0.45***	0.29**
	(0.15)	(0.44)	(0.49)	(1.04)	(0.07)	(0.17)	(0.05)	(0.10)
Civil society participation	1.06***	1.35*	0.03***	0.02*	0.48***	0.48*	0.33***	0.19*
	(0.15)	(0.61)	(0.00)	(0.01)	(0.06)	(0.22)	(0.44)	(0.10)
Number of alliances	−0.00	−0.01	−0.01	−0.05***	−0.00	−0.01**	−0.00	−0.00
	(0.00)	(0.01)	(0.01)	(0.01)	(0.00)	(0.00)	(0.00)	(0.00)
Trade openness	−0.00	−0.00	−0.00	−0.00	0.00	−0.00	0.00	−0.00
	(0.00)	(0.00)	(0.00)	(0.00)	(0.00)	(0.00)	(0.00)	(0.00)
Corruption	−0.30***	−0.31	−1.25***	−1.13**	−0.23***	−0.17*	−0.20***	−0.10*
	(0.07)	(0.18)	(0.24)	(0.43)	(0.03)	(0.07)	(0.03)	(0.05)
Quality of government	0.00	−0.19	0.16	−0.33	0.15***	−0.02	0.15***	0.09
	(0.12)	(0.44)	(0.39)	(0.95)	(0.04)	(0.12)	(0.03)	(0.07)

SOURCES: Center for Systemic Peace, undated; Coppedge et al., 2020; Coppedge et al., 2021; Freedom House, undated.
NOTES: *$p < 0.05$; **$p < 0.01$; ***$p < 0.001$. Standard errors in parentheses.

CHAPTER FOUR

Case Studies

We now turn to Asia to discover the factors that are relevant for democratization in this region, including those that could become policy instruments and attract external support. We expect deviations from global trends. Consider income growth. Unlike several authoritarian countries in eastern Europe and Africa, many Asian countries have experienced high income growth during times of authoritarianism. The citizens of these countries might be less disposed to accept democracy in return for growth, particularly if past experiences with democratization were accompanied by civic unrest or similar events.

We also expect to discover unique factors, such as ethnic composition, military involvement in politics, and location relative to hegemonistic countries in the neighborhood.

We selected four Asia-Pacific states at different stages of democratization for our case studies: a liberal democracy (Taiwan), a closed autocracy (Thailand), an electoral autocracy (Malaysia), and an electoral democracy (Sri Lanka). The case studies were developed via analysis and interviews with policymakers and policy analysts on the topic of democratization in the countries studied. The interviews were conducted in person and via video teleconference. For each case study, we discuss the four types of factors arising from the literature review and the statistical analysis—socioeconomic, political and governance, civil society, and international linkages—as well as unique country-specific factors.

Taiwan

From its formation in 1949 to the mid-1980s, Taiwan was a state under martial law administered by the Kuomintang (KMT).[1] Since then, Taiwan has rapidly evolved, starting with the formation of new political parties in the mid-1980s, to become the vibrant democracy that it is today (Figure 4.1). This evolution has occurred through a series of gradual and peaceful reforms: the lifting of martial law and the formation of the Democratic Progressive Party (DPP) in 1986, which led to a 6-point increase in Taiwan's score on the Polity IV index; the first direct elections for the Legislative Yuan in 1992 (an 8-point score); and the first competitive presidential election in 1996 (a score of 9 in 1997).[2] Taiwan achieved the maximum democracy score in 2004, after the second successful bid of DPP's Chen Shui-bian, and has kept it ever since. Freedom House has awarded Taiwan the "free" status every year since 1996.[3]

---

[1] The *Kuomintang*, translated as the *Chinese Nationalist Party*, moved the seat of the Republic of China to Taiwan in 1949 after being defeated in the civil war in China.

[2] According to the Center for Systemic Peace,

> [t]he "Polity Score" captures this regime authority spectrum on a 21-[point] scale ranging from -10 (hereditary monarchy) to +10 (consolidated democracy). The Polity scores can also be converted into regime categories in a suggested three part categorization of "autocracies" (-10 to -6), "anocracies" (-5 to +5 and three special values: -66, -77 and -88), and "democracies" (+6 to +10). (Center for Systemic Peace, undated)

[3] Coppedge et al., 2021; Freedom House, undated.

FIGURE 4.1

The Evolution of Democracy in Taiwan

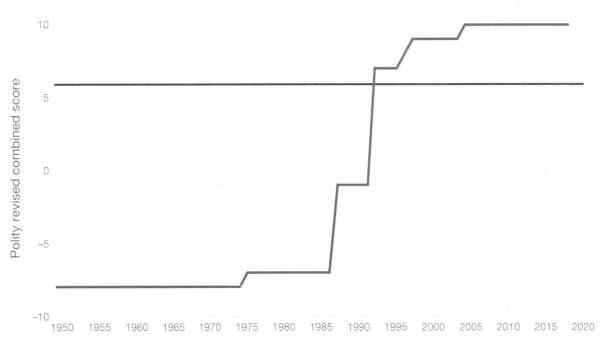

SOURCE: Created with data from Coppedge et al., 2021.
NOTE: A score above six (marked by the red line) corresponds to democracy.

The Economist Intelligence Unit's 2020 ranking upgraded Taiwan from a "flawed democracy" to a "full democracy," which put it in 11th place globally.[4] Moreover, Taiwan's exemplary conduct in its 2020 elections has earned it a maximum score in the "electoral process and pluralism" index component and near-top scores in the categories of "functioning of government" and "civil liberties" (Figure 4.2). Overall, the elections are competitive, free, and fair, and the defeated party has conceded the results in every election since 1992.

Next, we will explore the different factors that might have contributed to Taiwan's democratic transition, as well as the potential pitfalls going forward.

Socioeconomic Factors

GDP growth in the authoritarian period (1951–1986) averaged 6.1 percent per year, driven by macroeconomic stability and mercantilist industrial policies.[5] Democratic reforms in 1986 were followed by continued growth; growth averaged 6.4 percent between 1987 and 1996. Democratic consolidation after 1996 coincided with more-moderate average growth (3.3 percent) between 1997 and 2018.[6] Economic growth was accompanied by low income inequality (Figure 4.3).

---

[4] Economist Intelligence Unit, 2021.

[5] Cheng-Tian Kuo, *Global Competitiveness and Industrial Growth in Taiwan and the Philippines*, Pittsburgh, Pa.: University of Pittsburgh Press, 1995, as quoted in Stephan Haggard, *Developmental States*, Cambridge, United Kingdom: Cambridge University Press, 2018, p. 23.

[6] Computation is based on GDP per capita growth rates reported by the Maddison Project (Jutta Bolt and Jan Luiten van Zanden, *The Maddison Project: Maddison Style Estimates of the Evolution of the World Economy: A New 2020 Update*, Groningen, The Netherlands: University of Groningen, WP-15, October 2020).

FIGURE 4.2
Democracy in Taiwan in Recent Years

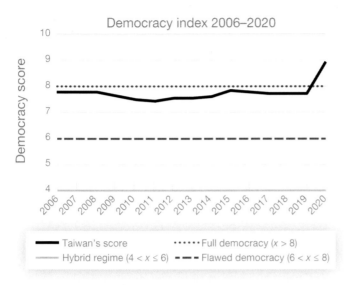

Democracy index 2006–2020

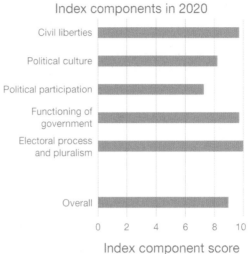

Index components in 2020

SOURCE: Created with data from Economist Intelligence Unit, 2021.
NOTE: A "full democracy" corresponds to an overall score of 8 or higher.

FIGURE 4.3
Economic Growth and Inequality in Taiwan

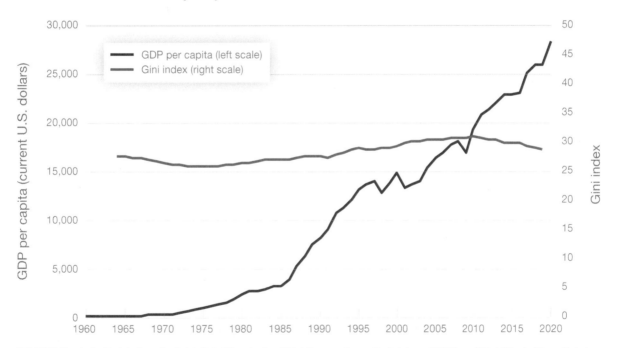

SOURCE: Created with data from Frederick Solt, "Standardized World Income Inequality Database," 2020; and World Bank, "Open Data," database, undated a.

Urbanization rose from 26.8 percent in 1950 to 59.5 percent in 1986 and 78.9 percent in 2020. Higher education also expanded tremendously. University student enrollment increased 52-fold between 1950 and 1986, then tripled between 1986 and 2012. As of 2021, nearly 70 percent of young people in the 18–22 age cohort are enrolled in higher education institutions.[7] Students have been active in civic life. For example, students initially organized the Sunflower Movement that contributed to the defeat of the KMT in the midterm elections in 2014 and the presidential election in 2016.[8] A demographic issue on the horizon is Taiwan's precipitously declining total fertility rate—at 1.07 as of 2021, one of the world's lowest—with consequences for migration, elder care, and financial stability that could affect democratic stability.

Political and Governance Factors

Since 1994, Taiwan has had seven presidential and 11 parliamentary elections, with voter turnout above 70 percent for most presidential elections and above 60 percent in parliamentary elections (Figure 4.4). The KMT and the DPP dominate politics. The early years of democratization in Taiwan gave voice to those opposed to the KMT positions on mainland relations and domestic issues, such as distributional justice and corruption. Over time, the KMT and the DPP have hewed to the middle on domestic issues but have remained split on positions vis-à-vis mainland policy and the meaning of an independent Taiwan polity. Despite this trend, however, the two main parties continue to seek out centrist voters and avoid polarization. Mainland

FIGURE 4.4
Voter Turnout in Presidential and Parliamentary Elections in Taiwan

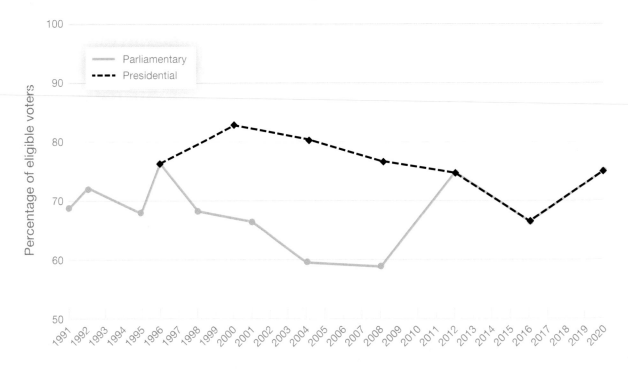

---

[7] Chuing Prudence Chou, "Education in Taiwan: Taiwan's Colleges and Universities," Brookings Institution, November 12, 2014.

[8] Thomas Gold and Sebastian Veg, eds., *Sunflowers and Umbrellas: Social Movements, Expressive Practices, and Political Culture in Taiwan and Hong Kong*, Berkeley, Calif.: Institute of East Asian Studies, University of California, Berkeley, 2020, p. 101.

policy is important but not decisive in political outcomes. As of 2021, the KMT remains a potent political force but struggles with the new reality of cross-strait relations and the shift in Chinese-U.S. relations.[9]

Between 1949 and the mid-1980s, the judiciary did not impose significant constraints on the executive because of martial law.[10] The judicial independence reforms were pioneered by the Room 303 judges from the Taizhong District Court in 1993 and included reforms of case assignment and review, the Personnel Review Council, the judicial budget, and detention. According to interviewees, the judiciary is now considered to be one of the key pillars in the continued success of Taiwan's democracy.

The military was the main force that was used to maintain internal security through martial law. Active-duty generals frequently held key positions in the administration. But the armed forces did not resist the democratization of the 1990s and accepted the results of the 2000 presidential election that elected the DPP's Chen Shui-bian. Possible explanations behind Taiwan's progress toward civilian supremacy include the external threat from China that helped unite the political objectives of the military and the civilian government, skilled leadership by presidents Chiang Ching-kuo and Lee Teng-hui, and public pressure from the legislature and the media.[11]

International Linkages

International economic agreements did not play an important role in the democratization of Taiwan. Most of its bilateral and multilateral trade agreements were concluded after the democratic reforms in the 1980s. Taiwan joined the Asia-Pacific Economic Cooperation (APEC) in 1991 and the World Trade Organization in 2002, and it concluded four bilateral trade agreements and several agreements on economic cooperation in the 2010s.

The economic and security relationships with the United States may have indirectly supported democratization. Initially, the United States helped legitimize KMT rule.[12] Although the United States did not exert strong pressure on the KMT to improve its human rights record, over time, Taiwan's supporters in the United States became increasingly frustrated by martial law and may have contributed to President Chiang Ching-kuo's decision to lift martial law in 1987.[13]

Taiwan's most important associational membership is APEC, an ASEAN-inspired economic cooperation zone that includes Pacific Rim states. APEC's benefits to Taiwan are geopolitical, lending it legitimacy in the region. There is no support for democratization in APEC.

Although Taiwan's relationship with mainland China remains its most significant challenge, the economic ties between China and Taiwan are deep and transcend administration type. China is, by far, Taiwan's largest trading partner and is a recipient of large foreign direct investment flows from Taiwan. According to interviewees, the intensifying competition between the United States and China increasingly puts Taiwan in a position in which maintaining close economic ties with China, especially in critical technologies, such

---

[9] Wei-chin Lee, ed., *Taiwan's Political Re-Alignment and Diplomatic Challenges*, Cham, Switzerland: Springer Nature, Springer International Publishing AG, Palgrave Macmillan, 2019, pp. 35–37.

[10] Wen-Chen Chang, "Courts and Judicial Reform in Taiwan: Gradual Transformations Towards the Guardian of Constitutionalism and Rule of Law," in *Asian Courts in Context*, Cambridge, United Kingdom: Cambridge University Press, 2014.

[11] M. Taylor Fravel, "Towards Civilian Supremacy: Civil-Military Relations in Taiwan's Democratization," *Armed Forces & Society*, Vol. 29, No. 1, Fall 2002, p. 58.

[12] Murray A. Rubinstein, ed., *Taiwan: A New History*, Abingdon, United Kingdom, and New York: Routledge, 2015, p. 325.

[13] Yangsun Chou and Andrew J. Nathan, "Democratizing Transition in Taiwan," *Asian Survey*, Vol. 27, No. 3, March 1987, p. 295; and interviewees.

as semiconductors, is colliding with Taiwan's drive to strengthen security and political ties with the United States.

Civil Society Factors

Civil society has been an important force behind Taiwan's democratization. One of the most remarkable features of Taiwanese civil society is its ability to scrutinize the government in a nonpartisan manner, as was the case when many DPP allies in the progressive camp organized large-scale demonstrations against President Chen Shui-bian (also a DPP member) after he was embroiled in a corruption scandal.[14] Most recently, the Sunflower Movement was the latest in a long series of social movements that contributed to Taiwan's democratization and identity formation.

Another distinctive factor in Taiwan's civil society and political life is the high level of women's political representation—a result driven by the implementation of gender quotas since the 1950s. Further reforms of the quota systems during the democratization process in the 1990s and 2000s were driven by women's organizations.[15]

Summary

A key finding is that the Taiwanese view democratization as having happened through their struggles and sacrifices rather than through outside support. With regard to the effect of Chinese policy on Taiwan's democracy, the Taiwanese value the economic relationship and believe that China does too—not only for the economic benefits but for building Taiwan's dependence on China. There is concern that such dependence could compromise Taiwan's security relations with the United States. This relationship is particularly important to Taiwan in light of China's growing assertiveness regarding its claims on Taiwan.

In the past, the Taiwanese did not believe that China wanted to impose an authoritarian system on Taiwan. This perception changed in 2020 and could change the level of polarization in the future about how to deal with China, which could lead to a change in the acceptance of the values inherent in strong people-to-people exchanges between the two countries.

Thailand

Thailand established a constitutional monarchy in 1932, placing the king as the titular head of state and the head of the armed forces and giving the king the divine right to be the guardian of the country's main faith, Buddhism. A unitary system of governance is exercised by the elected National Assembly, and executive power is vested in the prime minister and the cabinet.

A strictly enforced lèse-majesté law, under which it is illegal to defame, insult, or threaten the royal family's immediate members, is supported by the military, which has used it to suppress democratization. In return, the king is promoted as a figure worthy of veneration.

Since 1932, Thailand has had 20 constitutions and endured 12 military coups, the latest occurring in 2014 and still in administration at the time of writing (2021). The Polity Project classified Thailand as an autocracy in most years between 1958 and 1976 (Figure 4.5).

---

[14] Tun-jen Cheng and Yun-han Chu, eds., *Routledge Handbook of Democratization in East Asia*, New York: Routledge, 2017, p. 75.

[15] Chang-Ling Huang, "Gender Quotas in Taiwan: The Impact of Global Diffusion," *Politics & Gender*, Vol. 11, No. 1, March 2015.

FIGURE 4.5

The Development and Setbacks of Democracy in Thailand

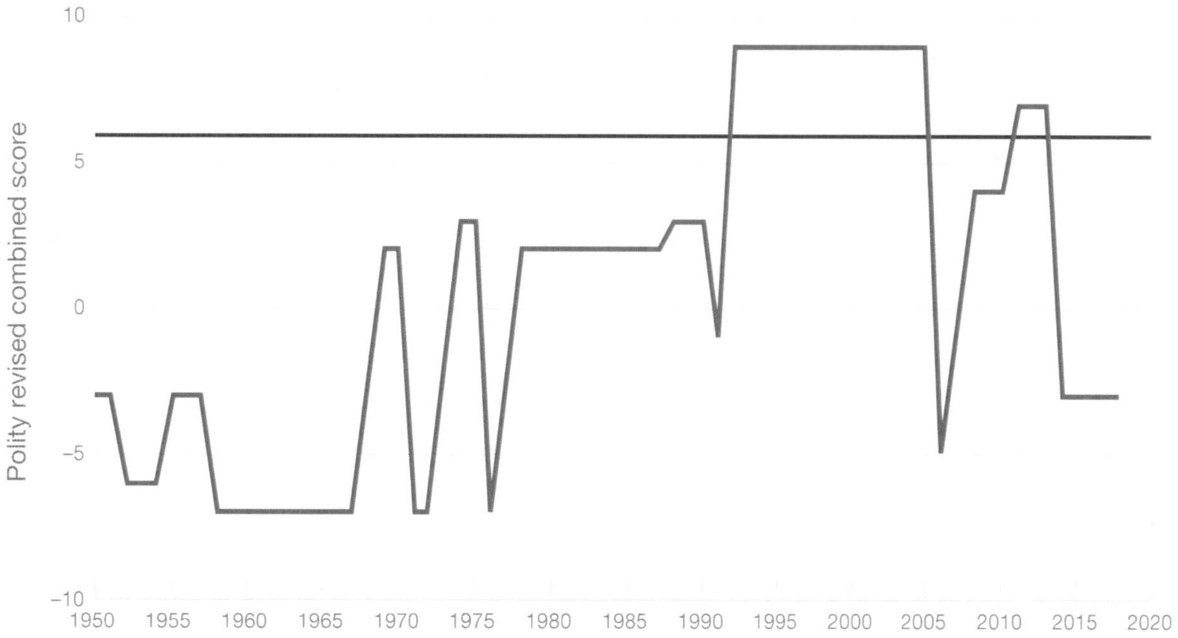

SOURCE: Created with data from Coppedge et al., 2021.
NOTE: A score above six (marked by the red line) corresponds to democracy.

The first two decades following the World War II were dominated by military and interim regimes, interrupted by a brief democratic government between 1973 and 1976 and followed by a more liberal authoritarian regime in the 1980s under General Prem Tinsulanonda.

Gradual liberalization in the 1980s was once again interrupted in 1991 by an army coup. Protests and violence subsequently forced the army to cede control and led to a series of short-term coalitions. The period between 1992 and 2005, during which Thailand had a democracy score of 9 (on a scale from –10 to +10), was the most democratic in its modern history.[16]

The Economist Intelligence Unit rated Thailand as a "flawed democracy" in 2008 and a "hybrid regime" after 2014 (Figure 4.6, left panel). Elections were held in 2019 under a constitution written in 2017 that increased the role of the military and the monarchy in political governance.[17] There were widespread pro-democracy protests in 2020 that continued into 2021.[18] The Economist Intelligence Unit's 2020 assessment gave Thailand an overall score of 6, the lower border of a "flawed democracy." Thailand received relatively higher scores in the "electoral process and pluralism" and "political participation" index components and lower scores in the "functioning of government" and "civil liberties" components (Figure 4.6, right panel).

The causes of political instability in Thailand have been widely debated, ranging from royalist interpretations of "incompatibility of democratic institutions with Thailand's 'national culture'" to pro-democratic interpretations that see the root causes of instability as the government's continuous efforts to enforce "unity"

---

[16] Freedom House, "Freedom in the World 2020: Thailand," webpage, 2020.

[17] Freedom House, 2020.

[18] Joel Selway, "Thailand's National Moment: Protests in a Continuing Battle over Nationalism," Brookings Institution, November 2, 2020.

FIGURE 4.6

The Evolution and the Current State of Democracy in Thailand

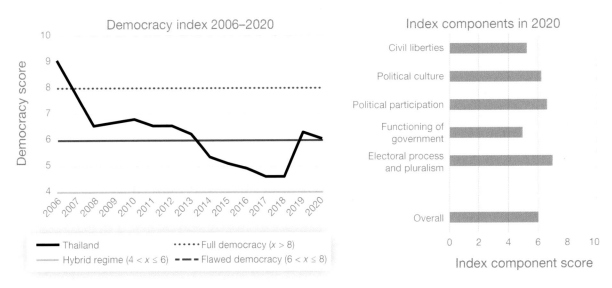

SOURCE: Created with data from Economist Intelligence Unit, 2021.
NOTE: A "full democracy" corresponds to an overall score of 8 or higher.

despite the increasing cultural and social diversity of the country.[19] Most observers note that Thailand's internal contradictions are driven by the deep divisions between "old and new elites, the rich and the poor, urban and rural social forces, and different conceptions of Thailand's national identity."[20]

Socioeconomic Factors

In the decades after World War II, Thailand developed to ultimately become an upper-middle-income economy, with low income inequality and a rising middle class that benefited from the state's universal education and health policies (Figures 4.7 and 4.8).

However, these developments did not benefit democratization. For instance, Thailand witnessed five coups in the period of sustained economic growth between 1959 and 1986, when growth averaged 4.3 percent per year, which was twice the average growth rate for all low- and middle-income countries over the same period.[21]

Urbanization has progressed steadily and has been particularly marked since 2000, with potentially significant implications for Thailand's democracy. Rapid urbanization contributed to the formation of a new class of "urbanized villagers" that spanned across the urban and rural societies. These urbanized villagers, who had lower-middle-class income levels and aspirations, composed the main group of protesters in the 2010 Redshirt protests that escalated into violent confrontations with the military.[22]

---

[19] Federico Ferrara, *The Political Development of Modern Thailand*, Cambridge, United Kingdom: Cambridge University Press, 2015, pp. 269–270.

[20] Aurel Croissant and Philip Lorenz, *Comparative Politics of Southeast Asia: An Introduction to Governments and Political Regimes*, Cham, Switzerland: Springer, 2018, p. 295.

[21] Peter Warr, "Economic Development in Post-War Thailand," in Pavin Chachavalpongpun, ed., *Routledge Handbook of Contemporary Thailand*, London: Routledge, 2019.

[22] Naruemon Thabchumpon and Duncan McCargo, "Urbanized Villagers in the 2010 Thai Redshirt Protests: Not Just Poor Farmers?" *Asian Survey*, Vol. 51, No. 6, November 2011, p. 999.

FIGURE 4.7

Economic Growth, Inequality, and Coups in Thailand, 1960–2020

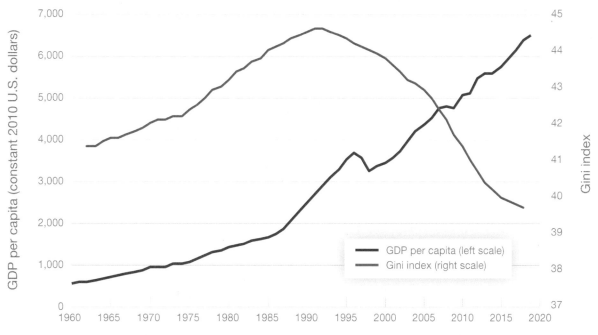

SOURCE: Created with data from Frederick Solt, 2020; and World Bank, undated a.

FIGURE 4.8

Average Years of Education Among Citizens Older Than 15 in Selected Asian Countries

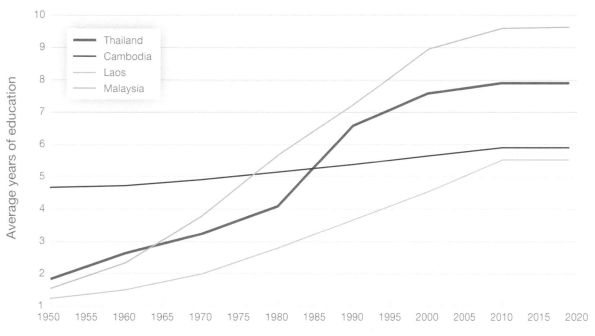

SOURCE: Created with data from Clio Infra, "Datasets," webpage, undated.

Political and Governance Factors

According to interviewees, the quality of the bureaucracy and the judiciary have been key contributors to economic growth in Thailand so that, even during periods of political instability, Thailand has possessed a technically competent government. Doner's analysis of Thailand's economic growth shows how elites sought to deliver economic growth to legitimize authoritarian rule.[23]

The military has played an outsized role in the country's political life. According to Neher,

> [t]he multi-party system that developed in the 1970s continued to feature weak formal structures and a lack of ideology and platform. Elections have not always been an effective barometer of democracy in Thailand because they have been manipulated by the rulers to legitimize their rule or by the military to legitimize a coup.[24]

Rising voter participation has been an important structural factor in Thailand's political life (Figure 4.9). Educated young Thais believe that elections are a key mechanism of democracy.[25]

Earlier civil society movements were largely rural,[26] but this is changing. Since the coup of 2014, a realization that military rule does not meet the aspirations of the rising population of the urban Thai middle class has led to civil society movements that are pro-democracy and urban. The rise of the now-dissolved Future

FIGURE 4.9
Voter Turnout in Parliamentary Elections in Thailand

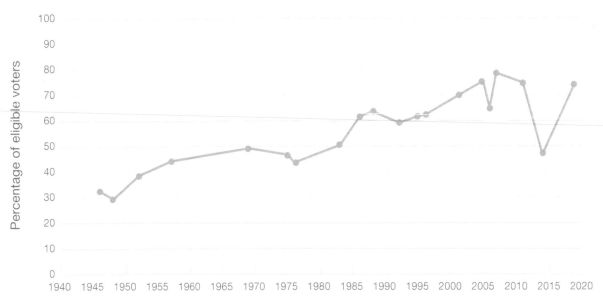

SOURCE: Created with 2021 data from International Institute for Democracy and Electoral Assistance, undated.

---

[23] Richard F. Doner, "The Politics of Uneven Development: Thailand's Economic Growth in Comparative Perspective," New York: Cambridge University Press, 2009.

[24] Clark Neher, "Democratization in Thailand," *Asian Affairs*, Vol. 21, No. 4, Winter 1995, p. 201.

[25] Chulanee Thianthai, "Perceptions of Democracy Among Thai Adolescents," Freiburg, Germany: Southeast Asian Studies at the University of Freiburg, Occasional Paper No. 9, February 2012.

[26] Robert B. Albritton and Thawilwadee Bureekul, "Civil Society and the Consolidation of Democracy in Thailand," Taipei: Asian Barometer Project Office, National Taiwan University and Academia Sinica, Working Paper No. 4, November 2002, pp. 6–9.

Forward Party (under contentious circumstances)[27] is a reflection of the rise in a pro-democratic urban civil society in Thailand.[28]

International Linkages

Thailand is a relatively rich country in Southeast Asia, ranking second in GDP and fourth in per capita GDP. It is the largest spender on defense in ASEAN. These factors, along with its military alliance with the United States, have given it a large degree of influence within ASEAN.

Thailand has a military alliance with the United States dating back to 1954.[29] The United States condemned the 2014 military coup but continued to maintain strong defense relations with Thailand's military. In recent years, even as Thailand has slipped further into authoritarianism, the United States—driven by its strategic competition with China—has sought closer relations with Thailand.[30] However, this does not imply that the U.S. role in Thailand's defense relations spills over into domestic politics. Nor does China seem to be playing a role in Thailand's domestic politics, despite deepening defense and economic ties with Thailand.

Over time, China might dominate Thailand's international relations. Thailand is part of the Belt and Road Initiative (BRI), China's expansive infrastructure and loan program, and has signed onto the rail network that China is seeking to build with its six southwestern neighbors.[31] The overall trend within Thailand is a gradual acceptance of a larger, long-term Chinese presence in the region, starting with an economic presence but undoubtedly moving toward strategic influence. This is unlikely to disturb the democratic deficit in Thailand.

Civil Society Factors

Nongovernmental organizations (NGOs) and civil society organizations have played an important role in Thai democratization and socioeconomic development, but this role has varied according to the political situation.[32] After the suppression of the student-led movements in 1976, civil society was largely silenced during the late 1970s. It slowly revived in the 1980s, a consequence of the transition from a military government to a parliamentary structure, supported by the expansion of international NGOs and religious organizations in Thailand.[33]

---

[27] Human Rights Watch, "Thailand: Court Dissolves Opposition Party," last updated February 22, 2020.

[28] Charlie Campbell, "'Thailand's Inconvenient Truth.' Why This Billionaire Is Risking It All to Back Reform of the Monarchy," *Time*, September 14, 2020.

[29] Bureau of East Asian and Pacific Affairs, U.S. Department of State, "U.S. Relations with Thailand," fact sheet, May 4, 2021.

[30] Zachary Abuza, "America Should Be Realistic About Its Alliance with Thailand," *War on the Rocks,* January 2, 2020.

[31] These are Cambodia, Laos, Malaysia, Singapore, Thailand, and Vietnam.

[32] Kanokwan Manorom, "NGOs and Civil Society in Thailand," in Pavin Chachavalpongpun, ed., *Routledge Handbook of Contemporary Thailand*, London: Routledge, 2019.

[33] Bencharat Sae Chua, "Thailand," in Akihiro Ogawa, ed., *Routledge Handbook of Civil Society in Asia*, London: Routledge, 2018, pp. 217–218.

Thailand has one of the region's highest internet penetration rates, at 75 percent.[34] Social media played an important role in the youth-led protests in 2020.[35] Losing freedom because of rising authoritarianism, the media earned a Freedom House ranking of 1 (out of 4) in 2020.[36]

Summary

Thailand's high economic growth, low economic inequality, rising urbanization, high education levels, and high voter participation suggest a readiness for democracy, evidenced by, among other events, the pro-democracy protests of 2020. Rising authoritarianism has been the result of the royalist-military alignment, legitimized to a large extent by the economic growth it has delivered.

Relations with larger powers and participation in ASEAN have not supported democratization. The best hope for democratization in Thailand is that even military leaders need the legitimacy of electoral politics to stay in power, which requires some compromise with pro-democracy forces, leading to opportunities for change.[37]

Sri Lanka

Sri Lanka, a colony under British rule from 1817 to 1948, went through a prolonged, although largely peaceful, struggle for independence in the first half of the 20th century. It was granted independence in 1948. Since then, fair elections have been held regularly. As of 2020, the Polity Project classifies Sri Lanka as a "weak democracy" (Figure 4.10), while the Economist Intelligence Unit's Democracy Index categorizes Sri Lanka as a "flawed democracy" (Figure 4.11) and ranks it 68th out of 167 countries, with its highest score in "electoral process and pluralism" (7 out of 10) and its lowest scores in "political participation" (5.56 out of 10) and "functioning of government" (5.71 out of 10).[38]

Historically, the levels of individual and political freedoms have varied, particularly for the minority Tamil population but also for other minority populations. Facing a long history of postcolonial discrimination from radical Sinhala Buddhist groups, a Tamil group, the Liberation Tigers of Tamil Eelam (LTTE), located in the northeast of the island state where Tamils are a majority, took up the Tamil cause and fought a war for secession from 1983 to 2009. At times, the government was brutal in its suppression of the LTTE and the civilian population that its members lived among.

Since 2009, when the LTTE was decisively defeated, the Tamil independence movement has died out. In its place is a rising nationalism among the majority Sinhala population that poses challenges for democracy in Sri Lanka. Until the 2015 national elections led to a change of government from the earlier Rajapaksa government, which represented the majority Sinhala Buddhist community, civic freedoms, such as free media, were severely restricted for all Sri Lankans. These were restored under the government of Maithripala Sirisena, who was in power until 2019 and lost the elections to a party led by Mahinda Rajapaksa. Since then, civic freedoms have once again been under pressure. However, the rise of nationalism since 2009 has not gone

---

[34] Simon Kemp, "Digital 2020: Thailand," presentation slides, DataReportal, February 18, 2020.

[35] Supalak Ganjanakhundee, "Thai Protests: A 1932 Revolution for the Social Media Generation," *South China Morning Post*, November 12, 2020.

[36] Freedom House, 2020.

[37] Panu Wongcha-um and Panarat Thepgumpanat, "How Thailand's Coup Leader Kept Power Through Election," Reuters, June 5, 2019.

[38] Center for Systemic Peace, undated; and Economist Intelligence Unit, 2021.

unchallenged. Sri Lanka has historically been a leader in social development and economic progress in South Asia, which may have given its population a sense of resilience and tolerance for diversity.

One of the external factors that has influenced Sri Lankan democracy is the role of India. The Tamil struggle against discrimination was supported by Tamil groups in India, and the Indian Army sought to stabilize

FIGURE 4.10

The State of Democracy in Sri Lanka Since 1948

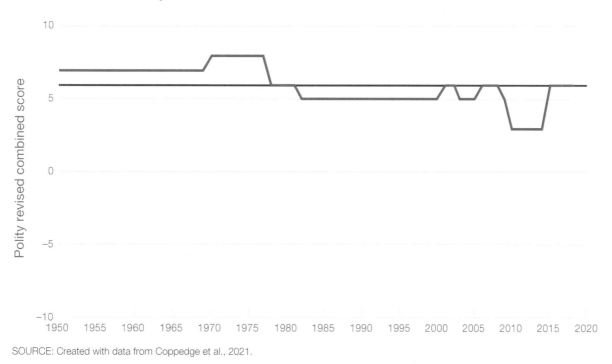

SOURCE: Created with data from Coppedge et al., 2021.

FIGURE 4.11

The Evolution and the Current State of Democracy in Sri Lanka

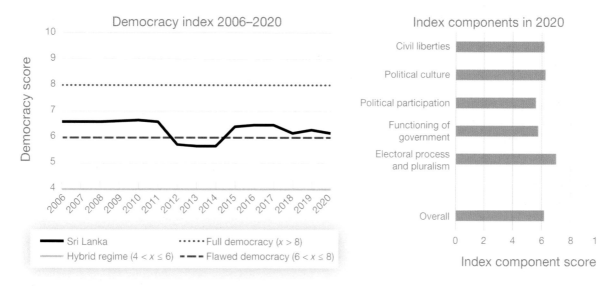

SOURCE: Created with data from Economist Intelligence Unit, 2021.
NOTE: A "full democracy" corresponds to an overall score of 8 or higher.

the situation in the Tamil areas of Sri Lanka through a peacekeeping force in a failed effort between 1987 and 1990. India's influence has since declined, although it is not absent. The Sirisena government (2015–2019), which was more accommodating of the Tamils than the predecessor Rajapaksa government, was supported by India. With the return of a Rajapaksa government to power in 2019, nationalist features have reemerged, and India's influence has declined.

Through the BRI, in which Sri Lanka is an active participant, China's influence has been rising. Sri Lanka is attracted to the BRI because of its desperate need for infrastructure. Because China is agnostic to regime type in its dealings under the BRI, its influence has continued through changes in government in Sri Lanka while seemingly having little effect on the state of democracy in the country.[39]

Socioeconomic Factors

Socioeconomic factors played a mixed role in Sri Lanka's journey toward democracy. Sri Lanka's rapid economic development—GDP growth averaged about 4.7 percent between 1962 and 2019 (Figure 4.12)—and decreasing inequality were supported by large investments in human capital development, in which Sri Lanka is an Asian leader. The country initially followed socialist policies that helped build human capital and led to the establishment of a vibrant civil society movement that continues to this day. Statism in economic policy was finally abandoned in 1977, after which GDP growth rates improved. During the 1977 reforms, policymakers refrained from the mercantilist policies that characterized much of East and Southeast Asia, making Sri Lanka one of the more open economies of Asia during this time.

FIGURE 4.12

Economic Growth and Inequality in Sri Lanka

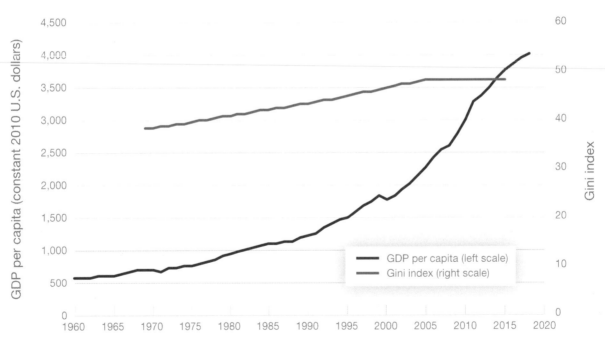

SOURCE: Created with data from Frederick Solt, 2020; and World Bank, undated a.

---

[39] China's influence has increased despite the controversy about Hambantota Port, a $1 billion BRI project that went bankrupt and was subsequently revived.

As mentioned, Sri Lanka is a leader in human capital development. The origins of this trend lie in Sri Lanka's socialist governments that ruled from 1948 until 1977. These governments invested heavily in basic civic and social services. By the late 1970s, there was widespread acceptance of the government's responsibility for providing free education, health care, and basic civic services. Subsequent governments were able to abandon statism in economic development but have retained the commitment to providing social services owing to popular resistance to change.

One of the negative outcomes of Sri Lanka's policy of free kindergarten-through-12th-grade education and unsubsidized tertiary education has been an unusual combination of high attainment up to the secondary level and a sharp decline thereafter. This is because the government did not have enough resources for tertiary education and has not been willing to encourage private provision, causing Sri Lanka to fall behind some of its neighbors in terms of average years of schooling (Figure 4.13).

Political and Governance Factors

Sri Lanka has had 16 parliamentary general elections and eight presidential elections since it became independent,[40] and high voter turnout has been a consistent feature of Sri Lanka's political life (Figure 4.14). But with rising nationalism, voting behavior is heavily influenced by the ethnic division between the Tamil, Muslim, and Christian minorities in alliance with liberal Sinhala factions on the one hand and the nationalistic Sinhala parties on the other.

FIGURE 4.13
Average Years of Education Among Citizens Older Than 15 in Selected Asian Countries

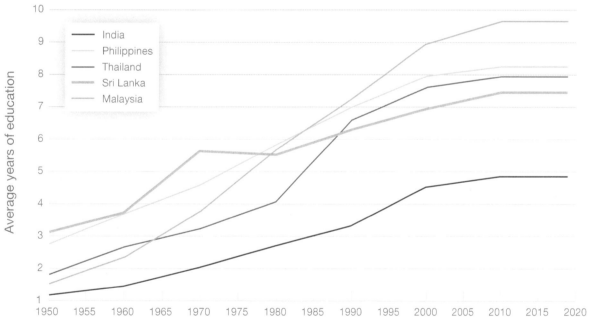

SOURCE: Created with data from Clio Infra, undated.

---

[40] Parliament of Sri Lanka, "Dates of Elections," webpage, last updated July 8, 2020.

FIGURE 4.14

Voter Turnout in Parliamentary Elections in Sri Lanka

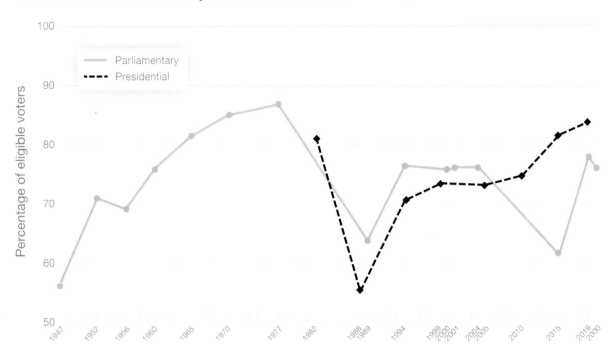

The judiciary and law enforcement played an important role in supporting democracy until the Tamil rebellion. Thereafter, both arms of the state have lost some of their independence under nationalist forces that agitated for more-repressive state actions in the face of a violent domestic insurrection.[41]

The military was subordinated to the civilian leadership through most of the pre-Tamil rebellion period, although there were two aborted military-led coups in 1962 and 1966.[42] However, the military's role increased with the LTTE's rebellion and in its aftermath. The final victory over the LTTE, in 2009, substantially raised awareness of the role of the military in civic life. In 2019, for the first time since becoming independent, Sri Lanka elected a military chief to become its president.

Looking ahead, Sri Lanka seems to be assured of the electoral process being conducted fairly, but the erosion of civic freedoms continues to be an issue.

International Linkages

Sri Lanka was a founding member of the South Asian Association for Regional Cooperation (SAARC) in 1985. Similar to ASEAN, SAARC has stayed clear of internal political issues, but, unlike ASEAN, it has been unable to promote good relations among member countries.

Sri Lanka signed free trade agreements with India in 1998 and Pakistan in 2005. While India and China are its two leading import markets for goods, Sri Lanka's exports, consisting mainly of textiles and primary goods, go largely to developed countries.[43] A second major source of exports is transshipment services. Sri

---

[41] Rohini Hensman, "Independent Judiciary and Rule of Law: Demolished in Sri Lanka," *Economic and Political Weekly*, Vol. 48, No. 9, March 2013.

[42] K. M. De Silva "Sri Lanka: Political-Military Relations," The Hague: Netherlands Institute of International Relations, Working Paper 3, November 2001.

[43] World Integrated Trade Solution, "Sri Lanka Trade," webpage, undated.

Lanka's port of Columbo is a major provider of transshipment services, mainly between India and the rest of the world. China is the largest foreign direct investor in Sri Lanka.[44] India's physical proximity to Sri Lanka (at its narrowest, the Palk Strait separates the mainland of the two countries by less than 40 miles) is seen in Sri Lanka as both an opportunity for economic growth and a threat to state and cultural sovereignty.[45]

Over the past two decades, Sri Lanka has become a venue for contests between India and China for political influence. From 1950 to 2000, India was the more dominant force and was seen to influence domestic issues, such as sending troops to calm the Tamil insurgency from 1987 to 1990. The rise in China's influence since then owes partly to its economic clout; it overtook India to become Sri Lanka's largest trading partner in 2017 and its largest lending source.[46]

There are well-founded concerns about the economic and security effects of U.S.-Chinese competition on Sri Lanka's international relations, as recent events have demonstrated.[47] This competition could indirectly affect the course of democracy in Sri Lanka because of rising Chinese influence, although there is no evidence of this at present. Sri Lanka's foreign relations portfolio is not entirely weighted in Asia. The nation has a long history of close relations with Nordic states, particularly Norway, based on foreign aid, environmental cooperation, governance, and, more recently, reconciliation of the Sinhala majority with the Tamil minority.

Civil Society Factors

Freedom of the press remains fragile in Sri Lanka. Sri Lanka has historically had one of the most vibrant environments for NGOs, particularly those in the area of grassroots social and economic development. Civil society organizations emerged as critical actors in the 1980s. The NGO sector in Sri Lanka is mainly represented through three types of organizations: (1) international NGOs that are working to alleviate the humanitarian situation after the ethnic conflict, (2) several large national NGOs working in conjunction with the government that are mainly concerned with poverty alleviation, and (3) a large number of smaller organizations involved in grassroots development.[48]

The end of the civil war in 2009 greatly increased the popularity of the Rajapaksa government, which used that popularity to suppress civil society organizations in the guise of seeking to improve order. There was a reversal of this trend when the Sirisena government was in office (2015–2019), only for another reversal to occur with the return of a Rajapaksa government. In recent years, the government has started regulating such organizations more closely, particularly those that receive funding from overseas.[49]

Summary

Sri Lanka's record of democracy in the postcolonial era is impressive. No other country in Asia matches its record of continuous, accurately counted elections. It is true that, in recent years, democracy has come under

---

[44] Rajiv Bhatia, Kunal Kulkarni, Lina Lee, and Shivani Gayakwad, "Chinese Investments in Sri Lanka," Gateway House, December 1, 2016.

[45] For example, India proposed building a bridge and a tunnel to connect the two countries, but this proposal was not accepted by Sri Lanka ("Sri Lankans Oppose Sea Bridge with India," *Asia Times*, December 23, 2015).

[46] P. K. Balachandran, "China Overtakes India as Sri Lanka's Largest Trading Partner," *The Citizen*, December 14, 2017.

[47] Akira Hayakawa, "US Yanks $480m Aid to Sri Lanka with Eye on China," Nikkei Asia, January 5, 2021.

[48] Nira Wickramasinghe, *Sri Lanka in the Modern Age: A History*, New York: Oxford University Press, 2014, p. 342.

[49] Freedom House, "Freedom in the World 2021: Sri Lanka," webpage, 2021; Reporters Without Borders, "Sri Lanka," webpage, undated.

severe strain, largely due to the rise of nationalist forces and the rising role of the military. This is a global trend. It afflicts Sri Lanka but is compounded by unique driving forces, such as the Tamil insurgency.

This trend does not bode well for Sri Lanka's future as a democracy. In Sri Lanka's neighborhood of South Asia, there is not much encouragement from pro-democracy forces; nationalist-driven threats to democracy are a feature in both India and Bangladesh, and the military has regularly challenged democracy in Pakistan.

With regard to societal characteristics, however, there is much to be encouraged about. Up to the recent past, the media and the judiciary in Sri Lanka were among the freest in Asia, and civil society working on grassroots issues was vibrant. Compared with its peers in South Asia, Sri Lanka has experienced high economic growth and human capital development. The ingredients on the ground seem to be sufficient to revive democracy, if given the chance.

With the state of Sri Lanka's international relations, reviving democracy in Sri Lanka appears to be possible only as a domestic project. Because the country is a place of contestation between autocratic China and quasi-democratic India, neither of which appears to be concerned about the state of democracy in Sri Lanka, one should not expect any changes in favor of democracy from these relationships.

Malaysia

Modern Malaysia came into being on September 16, 1963, as a federation of Malaya, Singapore, Sabah, and Sarawak that was ruled by a constitutional monarchy.[50] Two years later, Singapore was expelled from the Malaysian Federation in the aftermath of the race riots in 1964. Malaysia's democratic consolidation was interrupted by ethnic riots in 1969 that culminated with the suspension of the parliament and the imposition of emergency rule. Figure 4.15 shows the sharp fall of Malaysia's democracy score in 1969 from 10, which corresponds to consolidated democracy, to 1, which corresponds to anocracy.[51]

In 1971, the national emergency was lifted, and the electoral process was restarted. The ruling party during the emergency, the United Malays National Organization (UMNO), returned to power in the subsequent elections. It assumed an authoritarian stance, arguing that this was necessary to advance the economic interests of the long-depressed Malay community, by introducing preferential economic policies that benefited the Malays and other Bumiputera while preserving the political power of other groups. It did so through a multiethnic Barisan Nasional (National Front) coalition that incorporated the Malaysian Chinese Association, the Malaysian Indian Congress, and regional parties from Sabah and Sarawak.

In addition to communal and regional parties, there were parties with national and secular agendas, such as the Democratic Action Party (as of 2021, it is the largest single party in parliament, although its fortunes have varied with time). The appeal of these parties was limited during the period when Malaysia was poor because many Malays were attracted to appeals to Malay majoritarianism.

For UMNO, an alliance with other communal parties was a way to keep secular forces at bay and ameliorated, to an extent, UMNO's initially polarizing stance. For the Malaysian Chinese Association and other communal parties, the appeal of Barisan Nasional was that it insulated their constituents, to an extent, from accusations of separatism and wealth expropriation while ensuring that their constituents retained a share of national wealth by having a seat at the negotiating table when resources were differentially allocated to the Bumiputera.

When Malaysia was transitioning from a developing economy to a middle-income economy, the system worked well. The Malay population at large improved its human capital, and the elite Malays benefited from

---

[50] H. P. Lee, *Constitutional Conflicts in Contemporary Malaysia*, 2nd ed., Oxford: Oxford University Press, 2017, pp. 7–9.

[51] Center for Systemic Peace, undated.

FIGURE 4.15

Democracy in Malaysia

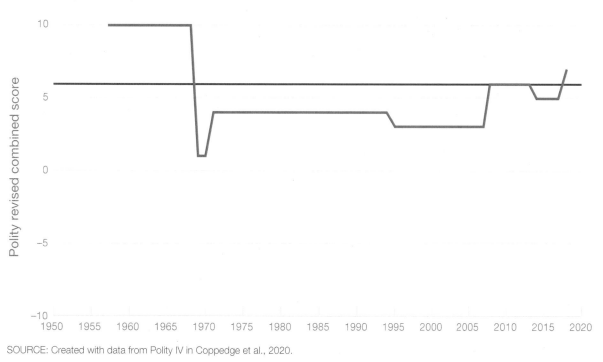

SOURCE: Created with data from Polity IV in Coppedge et al., 2020.

their privileged access to government-directed largesse. Meanwhile, the ethnic Chinese population, lacking such advantages, built a significant stake in the country's economy through entrepreneurship, supported over time by increasingly regional ethnic Chinese business networks.

In 2021, the old order has been challenged by the decline of the Malay business elite. Perhaps more importantly for democratization, the transition of Malaysia to upper-middle-income status since 1979 has improved the appeal of secular parties, thus enabling them to grow in popularity despite the burden of anocracy exercised by Barisan Nasional.[52]

Despite the overall improvement in democratic institutions and processes since 2005, limited civil liberties remain one of the key causes of Malaysia's inability to transition to a full democracy. Malaysia is categorized as a "flawed democracy" by the Economist Intelligence Unit. Its score has improved in recent years (Figure 4.16). Malaysia was ranked 39th of 167 countries and earned its highest score in the category of "electoral process and pluralism" and its lowest score in "civil liberties."[53] The improvement in its democracy score came after the introduction of laws enabling more-widespread political participation.

Socioeconomic Factors

Malaysia's rapid economic development—GDP growth averaged about 6.5 percent between 1961 and 2011—and decreasing inequality were means to justify the lack of political freedoms. The government adopted mercantilist economic policies to promote economic competitiveness and an outward-oriented economic

---

[52] According to the World Bank classification, Malaysia achieved the upper-middle-income status in 1979. It then receded to the lower-middle-income status in the subsequent years and regained upper-middle-income status in 1991 (Akira Suehiro, "Responses to the Middle-Income Trap in China, Malaysia, and Thailand," in Keiichi Tsunekawa and Yasuyuki Todo, eds., *Emerging States at Crossroads*, Singapore: Springer Nature, Springer Open, 2019).

[53] Economist Intelligence Unit, 2021.

FIGURE 4.16

The Evolution and the Current State of Democracy in Malaysia

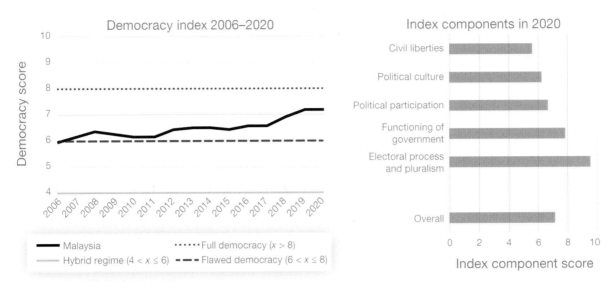

SOURCE: Created with data from Economist Intelligence Unit, 2021.
NOTE: A "full democracy" corresponds to an overall score of 8 or higher.

regime while restricting foreign direct investment and pursuing interethnic socioeconomic redistribution (Figure 4.17).[54]

At the same time, continuing economic growth has created a strong urban middle class and high expectations for the future, thus leading to a potential scenario in which decelerating growth might act as a catalyst for social change via increasing political participation, reforms, and democratization. In this sense, both continuing urbanization and the rise of the middle class are the structural factors that will underpin further democratization, according to interviewees.

Economic development and urbanization were accompanied by the improvement of education at all levels, making Malaysia a regional leader in human capital (Figure 4.18). The continual expansion of secondary and postsecondary education coincided with social activism and increased political participation, notably the Islamic revivalism movements in the late 1960s and 1970s and the Chinese educationist movements in the 1980s,[55] despite the imposition of the Universities and University Colleges Act of 1971, which prohibited students and faculty from expressing support for any political party or trade union.[56]

The quality and content of education programs have become issues of public debate in the context of democratic development, including the role of communal politics, according to interviewees. Some critics of the current system note that student activism tends to occur in educational environments that are dominated by the humanities, and not by science, technology, engineering, and mathematics programs.

[54] Greg Felker, "Malaysia's Development Strategies: Governing Distribution Through Growth," in Meredith L. Weiss, ed., *Routledge Handbook of Contemporary Malaysia*, Abingdon, United Kingdom: Routledge, 2014.

[55] Anantha Raman Govindasamy, "Social Movements in Contemporary Malaysia: The Cases of Bersih, Hindraf, and Perkasa," in Meredith L. Weiss, ed., *Routledge Handbook of Contemporary Malaysia*, Abingdon, United Kingdom, Routledge, 2014, p. 116.

[56] John Liu, "Civil Liberties in Contemporary Malaysia," in Meredith L. Weiss, ed., *Routledge Handbook of Contemporary Malaysia*, Abingdon, United Kingdom: Routledge, 2014, p. 292.

FIGURE 4.17

Economic Growth and Inequality in Malaysia

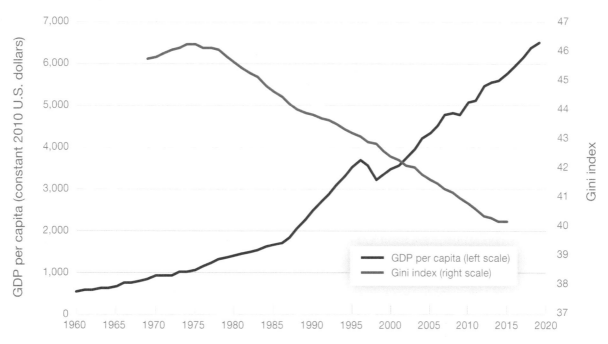

SOURCE: Created with data from Frederick Solt, 2020; and World Bank, undated a.

FIGURE 4.18

Average Years of Education Among Citizens Older Than 15 in Selected Asian Countries

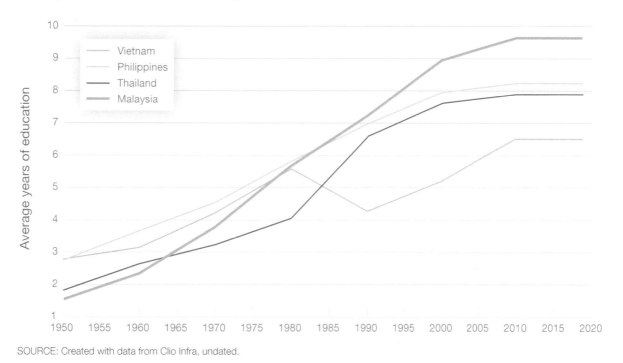

SOURCE: Created with data from Clio Infra, undated.

Political and Governance Factors

Malaysia has had 14 general elections since it became independent in 1957. High voter turnout has been a consistent feature of Malaysia's political life (Figure 4.19). The judiciary and law enforcement played a substantial role in underpinning the UMNO ruling party for decades. According to interviewees, with the advent of a more competitive era in Malaysian politics, the judiciary could play a key role in assuring free and fair elections.

The military has arguably been a less important factor in Malaysia's domestic politics because of the firm subordination of the military to the civilian leadership. Recently, there have been concerns about the use of the military to enforce lockdown measures during the emergency announced in early 2020.[57] The emergency measures were reintroduced in early 2021, suspending the parliament and any bids to seek a general election for at least six months.[58]

International Linkages

Given the focus on economic globalization, security agreements have been seen as less important since Malaysia became independent, according to interviewees. As a member of ASEAN, Malaysia promoted and benefited from ASEAN's neutral stance on regional and international affairs.

More recently, there have been concerns about the economic and security effects of U.S.-Chinese competition and their indirect effect on democracy in Malaysia. Malaysia is an active participant in the BRI. However, the country is avowedly anti-communist. (The Malaysian Communist Party was a key political actor at one time, with support from China, but was dissolved in 1989.) China is not seen to be an influential political

FIGURE 4.19
Voter Turnout in Parliamentary Elections in Malaysia

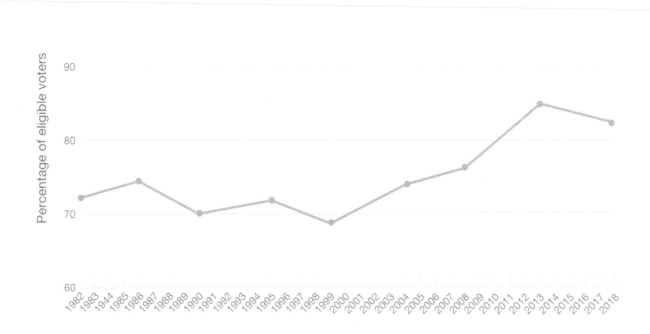

[57] Selam Gebrekidan, "For Autocrats, and Others, Coronavirus Is a Chance to Grab Even More Power," *New York Times*, last updated April 14, 2020.

[58] Eileen Ng, "Emergency Imposed in Malaysia over Virus Is Reprieve for PM," AP News, January 12, 2021.

player in Malaysia, despite occasional allegations that it exercises influence through the ethnic Chinese population in the country. This may be changing. In recent elections in Malaysia, China's preferences differed from those of the Chinese diaspora and appeared to influence the outcome.

Civil Society Factors

Civil liberties and civil society have played an important role in Malaysia's political life despite the government's long-standing position that it is necessary to limit some civil liberties for the sake of economic development and national security.[59]

The mainstream media has traditionally been seen as controlled by the government, while the digital revolution and the use of the internet have leveled the playing field in the media landscape and initially enabled the opposition, although the government was able to master the new technologies by the early 2010s.[60] At the same time, the proliferation of online media may have played a role in increasing polarization and disinformation.[61]

Summary

Malaysia's high economic growth, low and declining economic inequality, rising urbanization, high education levels, regular elections, and high voter participation coexisted for many decades with an electoral autocracy in which an alliance of largely communal parties delivered benefits for their favored constituents and used economic growth to justify the lack of freedoms. The state was particularly severe on freedom of expression, leading to an underdeveloped media and civil society sector that remains.

Unlike for many of Malaysia's Southeast Asian neighbors, the absence of a politically active military and strong federalism in Malaysia have ensured, even in the worst of times, a certain level of political participation by the public. This has made it easier for Malaysia to transition to higher levels of democracy, as has happened over the past 15 years, making Malaysia a rare case of rising democratization in Asia and in the world.

Malaysia has been active in ASEAN and has good relations with all of the ASEAN states, although occasional tensions in recent years have arisen over separatist movements in southern Thailand and the sharing of natural resources with Singapore. Outside ASEAN, Malaysia has no alliances or international agreements that could either help or impede democratization.

Looking ahead, the state of democracy in Malaysia will likely be driven by internal reforms. There are several legacy issues that need to be addressed through reforms. These include interracial policies, limits on freedom of expression, and the neglect of federalism.

---

[59] Liu, 2014, p. 290.

[60] Mustafa K. Anuar, "Muzzled: The Media in Mahathir's Malaysia," in Bridget Welsh, ed., *Reflections: The Mahathir Years*, Washington, D.C.: Johns Hopkins University Press, 2004; and Cherian George, *Contentious Journalism and the Internet: Towards Democratic Discourse in Malaysia and Singapore*, Singapore: Singapore University Press and Seattle: University of Washington Press, 2006.

[61] Quinton Temby, "Social Media and Polarization in the 'New Malaysia,'" Singapore: ISEAS—Yusof Ishak Institute, No. 21, March 27, 2020.

CHAPTER FIVE

Discussion and Conclusions

Summary of Findings

In this report, we studied democratization and the factors that influence it among small states in Asia. We also examined what policies strengthen democratization and the role that external actors can play.

We followed a three-stage approach: (1) a literature review to identify global and Asian trends in democratization and to identify influential factors from the economic, social, political, and geopolitical domains; (2) a statistical analysis to discover significant factors for Asia relative to global factors; and (3) interview-based case studies of four Asian states at different stages of democratization. These states are classified by the Regimes of the World index as a liberal democracy (Taiwan), a closed autocracy (Thailand), an electoral democracy (Sri Lanka), and an electoral autocracy (Malaysia). We used the case studies to examine the relevance of the factors that resulted from our statistical analysis and to discover determinants that were specific to the countries studied. Our findings are as follows:

- From our literature review and analysis of secondary data, we found that, globally and in Asia, there has been a reduction in the number of autocracies over time and, offsetting this, a rise in the number of partial democracies. The latter trend is due to both the retention of some autocratic institutions among new democracies and backsliding among previously liberal democracies.
- We explored modernization theory as a driver of democratization, leading to the identification of four classes of factors for further study: socioeconomic, political and governance, international linkages, and civil society participation.
- Our statistical modeling shows that several factors that are significantly associated with democratization globally also apply to Asia. These are the GDP per capita, human capital, and urbanization (socioeconomic factors); civil society participation and women's political empowerment (civil society factors); and independence of the judiciary, independence of subfederal units, and corruption (political and governance factors). Surprisingly, inequality, voter turnout, and quality of government, although significantly associated with democratization in our global analysis, are not significantly associated with democratization in Asia. External alliances (international linkages) are significant for Asia but are not globally significant. The GDP growth rate and trade openness are insignificant both globally and for Asia.
- Our country case studies show the following:
  - **Democratization:**
    - Democratic transitions—both upturns (i.e., to conditions of greater democracy) and downturns (i.e., to conditions of less democracy)—can occur without disruption to a country's normal political process, although this is not always the case. Malaysia and Sri Lanka are examples of such transitions.
    - However, democratization (both democratic consolidation and transitions to democracy) can face significant hurdles. Economic growth can be used to legitimize authoritarian rule, as in the cases

of Malaysia and Thailand, although such was not the case for Sri Lanka and Taiwan. Ethnic diversity, a hallmark of the typical Asian state, can hurt democratization, as in the cases of Malaysia and Sri Lanka. Malaysian politicians from the ethnic majority community created stable, communally based ruling coalitions with ethnic minority communities, crowding out secular parties. In Sri Lanka, suppression of the Tamil insurgency was accompanied by the rise of majoritarian governance. This has had negative implications for democratization.

- **Elections:** Even when elections are held regularly, they might not be fair, as the cases of Malaysia and Thailand show. Furthermore, voter participation does not correlate well with democratization in Asia. Voter participation in Asia tends to be high regardless of the state of democracy. Taiwan's and Malaysia's rates of voter participation regularly average over 70 percent. Thailand's voter turnout rate has been more volatile but still averages over 60 percent, as does Sri Lanka's.

- **The media:** Media freedom is closely related to the state of democracy. For instance, the Malaysian media was tightly controlled during the country's authoritarian period and has become freer, with greater democracy, in recent years. Thailand's media has become less free in recent years with the shift to autocracy. Sri Lanka's media lost significant freedom during the country's period of autocracy but regained its freedom once the autocratic period ended.

- **Civil society:** Civil society organizations flourish during periods of democratization, but their depth and resilience do not seem to be related to the state of democracy. This has been the case for Malaysia, Sri Lanka, and Taiwan. During episodes of democratic backsliding, civil society can play a critical role in keeping grassroots pro-democracy movements alive, as has been the case in all four countries studied.

- **The judiciary:** The judiciary is invariably an important player, but its role can both hurt democratization, as happened in Malaysia during UMNO rule and in Taiwan under martial law, and help it, as was Sri Lanka's experience until the Tamil insurgency and Taiwan's experience after the 1993 reforms.

- **External actors:**
  - External actors are usually marginal players in a country's democratization and are more effective when their role is noncoercive. Membership in regional and international institutions has not helped with democratization. Instead, in two cases, Malaysia and Thailand, a regional association may have legitimized authoritarianism by allowing autocratic leaders to promote concepts, such as "Asian values," that subordinated individual freedoms to the collective good.
  - Small Asian countries are of interest to large, influence-seeking regional and global players (primarily the United States and China on a pan-Asia basis and India in South Asia) for economic, diplomatic, and military purposes. The most significant change in this century is the role of China in Asian affairs, through regional associations, the BRI, and greater military preparedness and alliance-seeking. More recently, particularly during the administration of Chinese President Xi Jinping, China has used diplomacy both to build soft power and to influence domestic politics in other countries. In these respects, with the possible exception of the BRI, China is moving down a well-trodden path. In response to great-power initiatives for influence, small countries may adopt strategies ranging from accommodation to alliances with other countries to increase their bargaining power. With the exception of Malaysia, which uses its membership in ASEAN to gain bargaining power, the countries in our case studies have had to increasingly accommodate one or both of the larger powers that they face, with the attendant risk of confrontation with one of them. It is unlikely that this situation would lead the smaller countries to focus on democratization, and it might even hurt democratization by giving illiberal leadership an excuse for repressive behavior.

Policy Recommendations

Our conclusions suggest that a policy focus on economic growth, voter turnout, and external support is unlikely to help democratization. Furthermore, there are some positive influences that are natural structural changes that accompany development, such as urbanization and civil society participation, that policy can do little to influence. However, urbanization can be leveraged, and civil society can be a driver of change, particularly through grassroots movements.

There is much that policy reforms can influence. The key areas are human capital, regular elections, women's empowerment, independence of the judiciary and subfederal units, freedom of the media, corruption, and international linkages. The timing of policy intervention can also be important. For weak democracies, timing is key. The governments of such democracies should use democratic episodes to promote reforms. Of the cases studied, this could apply at present (2021) to Malaysia and Sri Lanka.

With regard to the role that external powers can play, regional associations in Asia have not been helpful in promoting democratization. The role of large, influence-seeking powers that are full democracies (primarily the United States) has historically been to compete with other large powers for military dominance. In consequence, the cause of democratization has not been helped. It might be better for sympathetic external actors that are full democracies to prioritize the "soft" areas mentioned above—such as promoting women's empowerment—and to build soft power rather than offer defense and diplomatic support, if they wish to help other countries democratize.

Of the countries studied, Taiwan is the only full democracy. Could it play a role in promoting democracy in other small countries? There are some potentially significant obstacles to the task of helping other countries democratize. The first is that Taiwan's relations with most other Asian states are economic and lack the political, social, and cultural connections through which soft power can be exerted. The second is the much longer shadow of U.S. influence in the region, which Taiwan is seen as allied to rather than independent from.

Taiwan's New Southbound Policy of 2016 might be an appropriate vehicle for public diplomacy. The policy envisages cooperation and exchange with the Asia-Pacific region in a variety of activities, including trade, tourism, education, and health care. If successful, the policy could lead to multidimensional people-to-people exchanges that could underpin the exercise of soft power.

Our policy recommendations can be summarized as follows:

1. The governments of fragile democracies should, during democratic upturns, seek to embed into law and practice the features that promote democratization. These include regular elections, investment in human capital, legal changes to empower women and strengthen the independence of civil society, the independence of the judiciary and subfederal units, the freedom of the media, and the tackling of corruption.
2. During democratic downturns, civil society should use grassroots movements and legal activism to ensure that as many pro-democracy features as were in practice during the prior democratic period are protected.
3. Sympathetic external actors that are full democracies should prioritize the "soft" areas mentioned above—such as promoting women's empowerment—rather than offer defense and diplomatic support, if they wish to help other countries democratize.

Summary of Findings from the Literature

Table A.1 indicates the effects of various factors on democracy globally and provides the studies that we reviewed for each factor.

TABLE A.1

Effects of Various Factors on Democracy Globally

Factor	Effect on Democracy	Studies
Economic development	Positive	Lipset, 1959 Przeworski et al., 2000
Income inequality	Negative	Iverson and Soskice, 2019 Lerner, 1958 Vanhanen, 2004
Civil society participation	Mixed	Alagappa, 2004 Haggard and Kaufman, 2016a Mercer, 2002
Women's empowerment	Positive	Fish, 2002 Huang, 2017 Waylen, 1994
Education	Positive	Almond and Verba, 2015 Barro, 1996
Urbanization	Positive	Lerner, 1958
Fixed national effects	Not applicable	Acemoglu and Robinson, 2006
Rationalism and self-expression	Positive	Inglehart and Welzel, 2010
Political freedoms	Positive	Arat, 1988 Bermeo, 2016 Przeworski, 2019
Free trade	Mixed	Autor et al., 2020 Colantone and Stanig, 2018 Liu and Ornelas, 2014 López-Córdova and Meissner, 2008 Pevehouse, 2002 Taniguchi, 2019
Diplomatic and military alliances and partnerships	Mixed	Lai and Reiter, 2000

Data and Model

Data

For the quantitative analysis, we primarily relied on the collection of data in the time-series Quality of Government (QoG) Standard data set, version Jan21, compiled by a team from the University of Gothenburg.[1] The QoG data set draws data on various aspects related to the quality of government from over 100 different sources, including the World Bank's World Development Indicators, the Organisation for Economic Cooperation and Development, and Eurostat.

The quantitative analysis was conducted on a sample of 169 countries over a 60-year period between 1960 and 2019. We excluded the observations from 2020 because of data availability issues in some World Development Indicators and the potential effects of the coronavirus pandemic. Our country selection process generally followed the process outlined in Teorell, 2010.[2]

We used four indicators to measure democracy. Our strategy was to apply the same set of regressions on each democracy index to examine the robustness of the results. The four democracy measures were as follows:

- *Polity revised combined score:* This variable ranges from –10 (strongly autocratic) to +10 (strongly democratic) and is computed by subtracting the autocracy score from the democracy score. The revised version of this variable is designed for use in time-series analysis. It covers 182 countries for the period between 1946 and 2017 and has a total of 9,574 observations.
- *V-Dem polyarchy index:* The polyarchy index is a composite democracy measure of the degree to which electoral democracy is achieved and is a weighted average of indexes that measure freedom of association, clean elections, freedom of expression, elected officials, and suffrage, as well as five-way multiplicative interactions between them. In the V-Dem conceptual scheme, electoral democracy is essential to any other conception of democracy. The index covers 183 countries between 1946 and 2017 and has a total of 9,788 observations. In our regressions, we multiplied the index by 100 to make the coefficients of the dependent variables more tractable.
- *Freedom House political rights index:* The political rights index measures the ability to freely participate in the political process, including the right to vote in legitimate elections, compete for public office, join political parties and organizations, and elect public representatives. The index ranges from 1 (most free) to 7 (least free), but, in our analysis, we recoded it from 1 (least free) to 7 (most free) for a more straight-

---

[1] Jan Teorell, Aksel Sundström, Sören Holmberg, Bo Rothstein, Natalia Alvarado Pachon, and Cem Mert Dalli, "The Quality of Government Standard Dataset," version Jan21, Gothenburg, Sweden: University of Gothenburg, Quality of Government Institute, 2021.

[2] Jan Teorell, *Determinants of Democratization: Explaining Regime Change in the World, 1972–2006*, Cambridge, United Kingdom: Cambridge University Press, 2010.

forward interpretation of the coefficient signs. It covers 195 countries and 14 related disputed territories between 1972 and 2017 and has a total of 8,002 observations.

- *Freedom House civil liberties index:* The civil liberties index measures the extent to which people have freedom of expression and beliefs, associational and organizational rights, rule of law, and personal autonomy without interference from the state. The index ranges from 1 (most free) to 7 (least free), but, in our analysis, we recoded it from 1 (least free) to 7 (most free) for ease of interpretation. The index covers 207 countries and territories between 1972 and 2017 (end years included) and has a total of 8,002 observations.

Table B.1 presents the descriptive statistics of the data. We used the following independent variables:

- *GDP per capita:* We calculated the GDP per capita by dividing the real GDP at constant 2011 national prices (in millions of 2011 U.S. dollars) by the country population (in millions). Both variables were taken from the Penn World Tables version 9.0 and cover 179 countries between 1950 and 2014.[3] We then applied a log transformation to the resulting measure.
- *GDP growth rate:* To compute the GDP growth rate, we used the real GDP at constant 2011 prices from the Penn World Tables version 9.0.
- *Trade openness:* We calculated trade openness by summing exports as a percentage of GDP and imports as a percentage of GDP. Both measures are provided by the World Development Indicators.[4]
- *Urbanization: Urban population* refers to people living in urban areas, as defined by national statistical offices. The data are collected and smoothed by the United Nations Population Division and provided via the World Development Indicators.
- *Independent judiciary:* We used a dummy variable coded 1 if there was an independent judiciary, according to information from the "Polity Executive Constraints" database; the data are sourced from the Political Constraints Dataset.[5]
- *Number of alliances:* This variable is the number of alliances in any given year. Data were provided by the Alliance Treaty Obligations and Provisions Project.[6]

TABLE B.1
Descriptive Statistics

Democracy Measure	Mean (standard deviation)	
	World	Asia
Polity revised combined score	0.89 (7.43)	−0.24 (7.08)
V-Dem polyarchy index	0.43 (0.28)	0.34 (0.24)
Freedom House political rights index	4.29 (2.23)	4.12 (2.14)
Freedom House civil liberties index	4.33 (1.94)	4.11 (1.84)

---

[3] Robert C. Feenstra, Robert Inklaar, and Marcel P. Timmer, "The Next Generation of the Penn World Table," *American Economic Review*, Vol. 105, No. 10, 2015.

[4] World Bank, "World Development Indicators," database, undated b.

[5] Monty G. Marshall, Ted Robert Gurr, and Keith Jaggers, *Polity IV Project: Political Regime Characteristics and Transitions, 1800–2016: Dataset Users' Manual*, Vienna, Va.: Center for Systemic Peace, 2017.

[6] Brett Ashley Leeds, Jeffrey M. Ritter, Sara McLaughlin Mitchell, and Andrew G. Long, "Alliance Treaty Obligations and Provisions, 1815–1944," *International Interactions*, Vol. 28, 2002.

- *Inequality:* We used the share of income of the richest 1 percent of the population as a measure of inequality. Data were provided by the World Inequality Database.[7]
- *Human capital index:* This index is based on the number of years of schooling and assumed returns,[8] and it is provided in the Penn World Tables version 9.0.
- *Women's political empowerment index:* This index is a composite measure that incorporates fundamental civil liberties, women's open discussion of political issues and participation in civil society organizations, and the descriptive representation of women in formal political positions. It covers 183 countries between 1946 and 2017.[9]
- *Civil society participation index:* This index is a composite measure of the following components: (1) consultation of leading civil society organizations (CSOs) by policymakers; (2) the representativeness of CSOs, including gender equity in representation; and (3) the involvement of the public in legislative candidate nomination processes.[10]

Model

To assess the contribution of different factors to the level of democracy, we used a pooled cross-section approach of the following form:

$$D_{it} = \beta_1 D_{it-1} + \beta_2 Y_{it-1} + \mu_t + \varepsilon_{it},$$

where D_{it} is the democracy score of country i in year t. D_{it-1} is the lagged value of the democracy score and is included to account for the persistent level of democracy and its mean-reverting dynamic. β_1 is a measure of the lagged effect. The main variable of interest is Y_{it-1}, and the parameter β_2 measures its impact on the democracy score. μ_t accounts for a full set of time effects, which are included to capture any shocks that are common to all countries. Finally, ε_{it} is the error term that captures all other omitted variables and has an expected value of 0 for all i and t.

This approach leads to consistent estimates of β_2 when the covariance between the lagged democracy score D_{it-1} and the error term ε_{it} equals 0 and the covariance between D_{it} and ε_{it} also equals 0. In other words, it assumes that no omitted variables are correlated with the independent variables in the model. Therefore, the results of this preliminary exercise should not be interpreted in the causal sense.

All regressions contain one lag of democracy, one lag of the dependent variable of interest, and time effects. The sample size varies depending on data availability, and the panel is unbalanced. Standard errors are robust against arbitrary heteroskedasticity and are clustered at the country level.

---

[7] World Inequality Database, homepage, undated.

[8] Robert J. Barro and Jong-Wha Lee, "A New Data Set of Educational Attainment in the World, 1950–2010," *Journal of Development Economics*, Vol. 104, April 2010.

[9] Aksel Sundström, Pamela Paxton, Yi-ting Wang, and Staffan I. Lindberg, "Women's Political Empowerment: A New Global Index, 1900–2012," *World Development*, Vol. 94, June 2017.

[10] Coppedge et al., 2021, p. 51.

Abbreviations

APEC	Asia-Pacific Economic Cooperation
ASEAN	Association of Southeast Asian Nations
BRI	Belt and Road Initiative
DPP	Democratic Progressive Party
GDP	gross domestic product
KMT	Kuomintang
LTTE	Liberation Tigers of Tamil Eelam
NGO	nongovernmental organization
SAARC	South Asian Association for Regional Cooperation
UMNO	United Malays National Organization
V-Dem	Varieties of Democracy

References

Abuza, Zachary, "America Should Be Realistic About Its Alliance with Thailand," *War on the Rocks*, January 2, 2020.

Acemoglu, Daron, and James A. Robinson, *Economic Origins of Dictatorship and Democracy*, New York: Cambridge University Press, 2006.

Alagappa, Muthiah, ed., *Civil Society and Political Change in Asia: Expanding and Contracting Democratic Space*, Stanford: Stanford University Press, 2004.

Albritton, Robert B., and Thawilwadee Bureekul, "Civil Society and the Consolidation of Democracy in Thailand," Taipei: Asian Barometer Project Office, National Taiwan University and Academia Sinica, Working Paper No. 4, November 2002.

Almond, Gabriel Abraham, and Sidney Verba, *The Civic Culture: Political Attitudes and Democracy in Five Nations*, Princeton, N.J.: Princeton University Press, 2015.

Andersson, Roland, John M. Quigley, and Mats Wilhelmsson, "Urbanization, Productivity, and Innovation: Evidence from Investment in Higher Education," *Journal of Urban Economics*, Vol. 66, No. 1, July 2009, pp. 2–15.

Anuar, Mustafa K., "Muzzled: The Media in Mahathir's Malaysia," in Bridget Welsh, ed., *Reflections: The Mahathir Years*, Washington, D.C.: Johns Hopkins University Press, 2004, pp. 486–493.

Arat, Zehra F., "Democracy and Economic Development: Modernization Theory revisited," *Comparative Politics*, Vol. 21, No. 1, October 1988, pp. 21–36.

Autor, David, David Dorn, Gordon Hanson, and Kaveh Majlesi, "Importing Political Polarization? The Electoral Consequences of Rising Trade Exposure," *American Economic Review*, Vol. 110, No. 10, 2020, pp. 3139–1383.

Balachandran, P. K., "China Overtakes India as Sri Lanka's Largest Trading Partner," *The Citizen*, December 14, 2017.

Barro, Robert J., "Democracy and Growth," *Journal of Economic Growth*, Vol. 1, No. 1, March 1996, pp. 1–27.

Barro, Robert J., and Jong-Wha Lee, "A New Data Set of Educational Attainment in the World, 1950–2010," *Journal of Development Economics*, Vol. 104, April 2010, pp. 184–198.

Bermeo, Nancy, "On Democratic Backsliding," *Journal of Democracy*, Vol. 27, No. 1, January 2016, pp. 5–19.

Bhatia, Rajiv, Kunal Kulkarni, Lina Lee, and Shivani Gayakwad, "Chinese Investments in Sri Lanka," Gateway House, December 1, 2016. As of June 24, 2021:
https://www.gatewayhouse.in/chinese-investments-sri-lanka-2/

Jutta Bolt and Jan Luiten van Zanden, The Maddison Project: Maddison Style Estimates of the Evolution of the World Economy: A New 2020 Update, Groningen, The Netherlands: University of Groningen, WP-15, October 2020. As of October 31, 2021:
https://www.rug.nl/ggdc/historicaldevelopment/maddison/releases/maddison-project-database-2020?lang=en

Bureau of East Asian and Pacific Affairs, U.S. Department of State, "U.S. Relations with Thailand," fact sheet, May 4, 2021. As of May 21, 2021:
https://www.state.gov/u-s-relations-with-thailand/

Campbell, Charlie, "'Thailand's Inconvenient Truth.' Why This Billionaire Is Risking It All to Back Reform of the Monarchy," *Time*, September 14, 2020.

Center for Systemic Peace, "The Polity Project," webpage, undated. As of September 16, 2021:
https://www.systemicpeace.org/polityproject.html

Chang, Wen-Chen, "Courts and Judicial Reform in Taiwan: Gradual Transformations Towards the Guardian of Constitutionalism and Rule of Law," in Jiunn-rong Yeh and Wen-Chen Chang, eds., *Asian Courts in Context*, Cambridge, United Kingdom: Cambridge University Press, 2014, pp. 143–182.

Cheng, Tun-jen, and Yun-han Chu, eds., *Routledge Handbook of Democratization in East Asia*, New York: Routledge, 2017.

Chou, Chuing Prudence, "Education in Taiwan: Taiwan's Colleges and Universities," Brookings Institution, November 12, 2014. As of June 22, 2021:
https://www.brookings.edu/opinions/education-in-taiwan-taiwans-colleges-and-universities/

Chou, Yangsun, and Andrew J. Nathan, "Democratizing Transition in Taiwan," *Asian Survey*, Vol. 27, No. 3, March 1987, pp. 277–299.

Clio Infra, "Datasets," webpage, undated. As of October 26, 2021:
https://clio-infra.eu/

Colantone, Italo, and Piero Stanig, "The Trade Origins of Economic Nationalism: Import Competition and Voting Behavior in Western Europe," *American Journal of Political Science*, Vol. 62, No. 4, October 2018, pp. 936–953.

Coleman, James S., "Conclusion: The Political Systems of the Developing Areas," in Gabriel Abraham Almond and James Smoot Coleman, eds., *The Politics of the Developing Areas*, Princeton, N.J.: Princeton University Press, 1960, pp. 532–576.

Coppedge, Michael, John Gerring, Carl Henrik Knutsen, Staffan I. Lindberg, Jan Teorell, David Altman, Michael Bernhard, Agnes Cornell, M. Steven Fish, Lisa Gastaldi, et al., *V-Dem Codebook*, version 11.1, Gothenburg, Sweden: University of Gothenburg, Varieties of Democracy Institute, Varieties of Democracy Project, March 2021.

Coppedge, Michael, John Gerring, Carl Henrik Knutsen, Staffan I. Lindberg, Jan Teorell, David Altman, Michael Bernhard, M. Steven Fish, Adam Glynn, Allen Hicken, et al., *V-Dem Codebook*, version 10, Gothenburg, Sweden: University of Gothenburg, Varieties of Democracy Institute, Varieties of Democracy Project, March 2020.

Croissant, Aurel, and Philip Lorenz, *Comparative Politics of Southeast Asia: An Introduction to Governments and Political Regimes*, Cham, Switzerland: Springer, 2018.

Dahl, Robert A., *Polyarchy: Participation and Opposition*, New Haven, Conn.: Yale University Press, 1971.

Dahl, Robert A., and Ian Shapiro, *On Democracy*, 2nd ed., New Haven, Conn.: Yale University Press, 2015.

De Silva, K. M., "Sri Lanka: Political-Military Relations," The Hague: Netherlands Institute of International Relations, Working Paper 3, November 2001.

Doner, Richard F., "The Politics of Uneven Development: Thailand's Economic Growth in Comparative Perspective," New York: Cambridge University Press, 2009.

Economist Intelligence Unit, *Democracy Index 2019: A Year of Democratic Setbacks and Popular Protest*, London, 2020.

———, *Democracy Index 2020: In Sickness and in Health?* London, 2021.

Feenstra, Robert C., Robert Inklaar, and Marcel P. Timmer, "The Next Generation of the Penn World Table," *American Economic Review*, Vol. 105, No. 10, 2015, pp. 3150–3182.

Felker, Greg, "Malaysia's Development Strategies: Governing Distribution Through Growth," in Meredith L. Weiss, ed., *Routledge Handbook of Contemporary Malaysia*, Abingdon, United Kingdom: Routledge, 2014, pp. 133–147.

Ferrara, Federico, *The Political Development of Modern Thailand*, Cambridge, United Kingdom: Cambridge University Press, 2015.

Fish, M. Steven, "Islam and Authoritarianism," *World Politics*, Vol. 55, October 2002, pp. 4–37.

Fravel, M. Taylor, "Towards Civilian Supremacy: Civil-Military Relations in Taiwan's Democratization," *Armed Forces & Society*, Vol. 29, No. 1, Fall 2002, pp. 57–84.

Freedom House, "Countries and Territories," webpage, undated. As of October 31, 2021:
https://freedomhouse.org/countries/freedom-world/scores

———, "Freedom in the World 2020: Thailand," webpage, 2020. As of January 13, 2021:
https://freedomhouse.org/country/thailand/freedom-world/2020

———, "Freedom in the World 2021: Sri Lanka," webpage, 2021. As of September 16, 2021:
https://freedomhouse.org/country/sri-lanka/freedom-world/2021

Ganjanakhundee, Supalak, "Thai Protests: A 1932 Revolution for the Social Media Generation," *South China Morning Post*, November 12, 2020.

Gebrekidan, Selam, "For Autocrats, and Others, Coronavirus Is a Chance to Grab Even More Power," *New York Times*, last updated April 14, 2020.

George, Cherian, *Contentious Journalism and the Internet: Towards Democratic Discourse in Malaysia and Singapore*, Singapore: Singapore University Press and Seattle: University of Washington Press, 2006.

Gold, Thomas, and Sebastian Veg, eds., *Sunflowers and Umbrellas: Social Movements, Expressive Practices, and Political Culture in Taiwan and Hong Kong*, Berkeley, Calif.: Institute of East Asian Studies, University of California, Berkeley, 2020.

Govindasamy, Anantha Raman, "Social Movements in Contemporary Malaysia: The Cases of Bersih, Hindraf, and Perkasa," in Meredith L. Weiss, ed., *Routledge Handbook of Contemporary Malaysia*, Abingdon, United Kingdom: Routledge, 2014, pp. 116–126.

Haggard, Stephan, *Developmental States*, Cambridge, United Kingdom: Cambridge University Press, 2018.

Haggard, Stephan, and Robert R. Kaufman, *Dictators and Democrats: Masses, Elites, and Regime Change*, Princeton, N.J.: Princeton University Press, 2016a.

———, "Democratization During the Third Wave," *Annual Review of Political Science*, Vol. 19, May 2016b, pp. 125–144.

Hanushek, Eric A., and Ludger Woessmann, "Education and Economic Growth," *Economics of Education*, 2010, pp. 60–67.

Hayakawa, Akira, "US Yanks $480m Aid to Sri Lanka with Eye on China," Nikkei Asia, January 5, 2021. As of September 7, 2021:
https://asia.nikkei.com/Politics/International-relations/US-yanks-480m-aid-to-Sri-Lanka-with-eye-on-China

Hensman, Rohini, "Independent Judiciary and Rule of Law: Demolished in Sri Lanka," *Economic and Political Weekly*, Vol. 48, No. 9, March 2013, pp. 16–19.

Huang, Chang-Ling, "Gender Quotas in Taiwan: The Impact of Global Diffusion," *Politics & Gender*, Vol. 11, No. 1, March 2015, pp. 207–217.

———, "Women's Political Empowerment," in Tun-jen Cheng and Yun-han Chu, eds., *Routledge Handbook of Democratization in East Asia*, London: Routledge, 2017, pp. 284–296.

Human Rights Watch, "Thailand: Court Dissolves Opposition Party," last updated February 22, 2020. As of May 24, 2021:
https://www.hrw.org/news/2020/02/22/thailand-court-dissolves-opposition-party

Inglehart, Ronald, and Christian Welzel, "Changing Mass Priorities: The Link Between Modernization and Democracy," *Perspectives on Politics*, Vol. 8, No. 2, June 2010, pp. 551–567.

International Institute for Democracy and Electoral Assistance, "Voter Turnout Database," undated. As of October 27, 2021:
https://www.idea.int/data-tools/data/voter-turnout

Iversen, Torben, and David Soskice, *Democracy and Prosperity: Reinventing Capitalism Through a Turbulent Century*, Princeton, N.J.: Princeton University Press, 2019.

Kanbur, Ravi, and Juzhong Zhuang, "Urbanization and Inequality in Asia," *Asian Development Review*, Vol. 30, No. 1, 2013, pp. 131–147.

Kemp, Simon, "Digital 2020: Thailand," presentation slides, DataReportal, February 18, 2020. As of May 24, 2021:
https://datareportal.com/reports/digital-2020-thailand

Kuo, Cheng-Tian, *Global Competitiveness and Industrial Growth in Taiwan and the Philippines*, Pittsburgh, Pa.: University of Pittsburgh Press, 1995.

Lai, Brian, and Dan Reiter, "Democracy, Political Similarity, and International Alliances, 1816–1992," *Journal of Conflict Resolution*, Vol. 44, No. 2, April 2000, pp. 203–227.

Lee, H. P., *Constitutional Conflicts in Contemporary Malaysia*, 2nd ed., Oxford: Oxford University Press, 2017.

Lee, Wei-chin, ed., *Taiwan's Political Re-Alignment and Diplomatic Challenges*, Cham, Switzerland: Springer Nature, Springer International Publishing AG, Palgrave Macmillan, 2019.

Leeds, Brett Ashley, Jeffrey M. Ritter, Sara McLaughlin Mitchell, and Andrew G. Long, "Alliance Treaty Obligations and Provisions, 1815–1944," *International Interactions*, Vol. 28, 2002, pp. 237–260.

Lerner, Daniel, *The Passing of Traditional Society: Modernizing the Middle East*, Glencoe, Ill.: Free Press, 1958.

Lipset, Seymour Martin, "Some Social Requisites of Democracy: Economic Development and Political Legitimacy," *American Political Science Review*, Vol. 53, No. 1, March 1959, pp. 69–105.

Liu, John, "Civil Liberties in Contemporary Malaysia," in Meredith L. Weiss, ed., *Routledge Handbook of Contemporary Malaysia*, Abingdon, United Kingdom: Routledge, 2014, pp. 290–301.

Liu, Xuepeng, and Emanuel Ornelas, "Free Trade Agreements and the Consolidation of Democracy," *American Economic Journal: Macroeconomics*, Vol. 6, No. 2, 2014, pp. 29–70.

López-Córdova, J. Ernesto, and Christopher M. Meissner, "The Impact of International Trade on Democracy: A Long-Run Perspective," *World Politics*, Vol. 60, No. 4, July 2008, pp. 539–575.

Lührmann, Anna, and Staffan I. Lindberg, "A Third Wave of Autocratization Is Here: What Is New About It?" *Democratization*, Vol. 26, No. 7, 2019, pp. 1095–1113.

Lührmann, Anna, Marcus Tannenberg, and Staffan I. Lindberg, "Regimes of the World (RoW): Opening New Avenues for the Comparative Study of Political Regimes," *Politics and Governance*, Vol. 6, No. 1, 2018, pp. 60–77.

Manorom, Kanokwan, "NGOs and Civil Society in Thailand," in Pavin Chachavalpongpun, ed., *Routledge Handbook of Contemporary Thailand*, London: Routledge, 2019, pp. 366–378.

Marshall, Monty G., and Ted Robert Gurr, *Polity 5: Political Regime Characteristics and Transitions, 1800–2018: Dataset Users' Manual*, Vienna, Va.: Center for Systemic Peace, April 23, 2020. As of September 16, 2021: http://www.systemicpeace.org/inscr/p5manualv2018.pdf

Marshall, Monty G., Ted Robert Gurr, and Keith Jaggers, *Polity IV Project: Political Regime Characteristics and Transitions, 1800–2016: Dataset Users' Manual*, Vienna, Va.: Center for Systemic Peace, 2017. As of October 31, 2021:
https://www.systemicpeace.org/inscr/p4manualv2016.pdf

Mercer, Claire, "NGOs, Civil Society and Democratization: A Critical Review of the Literature," *Progress in Development Studies*, Vol. 2, No. 1, January 1, 2002, pp. 5–22.

Neher, Clark, "Democratization in Thailand," *Asian Affairs*, Vol. 21, No. 4, Winter 1995, pp. 195–209.

Ng, Eileen, "Emergency Imposed in Malaysia over Virus Is Reprieve for PM," AP News, January 12, 2021. As of June 23, 2021:
https://apnews.com/article/kuala-lumpur-general-elections-elections-coronavirus-pandemic-malaysia-47c476998533a46ec9c34e067a7c7510

Parliament of Sri Lanka, "Dates of Elections," webpage, last updated July 8, 2020. As of September 7, 2021:
https://www.parliament.lk/dates-of-elections

Pevehouse, Jon C., "Democracy from the Outside-In? International Organizations and Democratization," *International Organization*, Vol. 56, No. 3, Summer 2002, pp. 515–549.

Przeworski, Adam, *Crises of Democracy*, Cambridge, United Kingdom: Cambridge University Press, 2019.

Przeworski, Adam, Michael E. Alvarez, José Antonio Cheibub, and Fernando Limongi, *Democracy and Development: Political Institutions and Well-Being in the World, 1950–1990*, Cambridge, United Kingdom: Cambridge University Press, 2000.

Reporters Without Borders, "Sri Lanka," webpage, undated. As of September 16, 2021:
https://rsf.org/en/sri-lanka

Rubinstein, Murray A., ed., *Taiwan: A New History*, Abingdon, United Kingdom, and New York: Routledge, 2015.

Sae Chua, Bencharat, "Thailand," in Akihiro Ogawa, ed., *Routledge Handbook of Civil Society in Asia*, London: Routledge, 2018, pp. 215–226.

Schedler, Andreas, "What Is Democratic Consolidation?" *Journal of Democracy*, Vol. 9, No. 2, April 1998, pp. 91–107.

Selway, Joel, "Thailand's National Moment: Protests in a Continuing Battle over Nationalism," Brookings Institution, November 2, 2020. As of May 21, 2021:
https://www.brookings.edu/blog/order-from-chaos/2020/11/02/
thailands-national-moment-protests-in-a-continuing-battle-over-nationalism/

Solt, Frederick, "Standardized World Income Inequality Database," 2020. As of October 26, 2021:
https://fsolt.org/swiid/

"Sri Lankans Oppose Sea Bridge with India," *Asia Times*, December 23, 2015.

Suehiro, Akira, "Responses to the Middle-Income Trap in China, Malaysia, and Thailand," in Keiichi Tsunekawa and Yasuyuki Todo, eds., *Emerging States at Crossroads*, Singapore: Springer Nature, Springer Open, 2019, pp. 27–48.

Sundström, Aksel, Pamela Paxton, Yi-ting Wang, and Staffan I. Lindberg, "Women's Political Empowerment: A New Global Index, 1900–2012," *World Development*, Vol. 94, June 2017, pp. 321–335.

Taniguchi, Mina, "The Effect of an Increase in Imports from China on Local Labor Markets in Japan," *Journal of the Japanese and International Economies*, Vol. 51, March 2019, pp. 1–18.

Temby, Quinton, "Social Media and Polarization in the 'New Malaysia,'" Singapore: ISEAS—Yusof Ishak Institute, No. 21, March 27, 2020. As of June 23, 2021:
https://www.iseas.edu.sg/wp-content/uploads/2020/02/ISEAS_Perspective_2020_21.pdf

Teorell, Jan, *Determinants of Democratization: Explaining Regime Change in the World, 1972–2006*, Cambridge, United Kingdom: Cambridge University Press, 2010.

Teorell, Jan, Michael Coppedge, Svend-Erik Skaaning, and Staffan I. Lindberg, "Measuring Electoral Democracy with V-Dem Data: Introducing a New Polyarchy Index," Gothenburg, Sweden: Varieties of Democracy Institute, Working Paper 25, March 2016.

Teorell, Jan, Aksel Sundström, Sören Holmberg, Bo Rothstein, Natalia Alvarado Pachon, and Cem Mert Dalli, "The Quality of Government Standard Dataset," version Jan21, Gothenburg, Sweden: University of Gothenburg, Quality of Government Institute, 2021. As of October 26, 2021:
http://www.qog.pol.gu.se doi:10.18157/qogstdjan21

Thabchumpon, Naruemon, and Duncan McCargo, "Urbanized Villagers in the 2010 Thai Redshirt Protests: Not Just Poor Farmers?" *Asian Survey*, Vol. 51, No. 6, November 2011, pp. 993–1018.

Thianthai, Chulanee, "Perceptions of Democracy Among Thai Adolescents," Freiburg, Germany: Southeast Asian Studies at the University of Freiburg, Occasional Paper No. 9, February 2012.

Treisman, Daniel, "Triggering Democracy," *Annals of Comparative Democratization*, Vol. 16, No. 3, September 2018, pp. 32–36.

Vanhanen, Tatu, *Democratization: A Comparative Analysis of 170 Countries*, London: Routledge, 2004.

Warr, Peter, "Economic Development of Post-War Thailand," in Pavin Chachavalpongpun, ed., *Routledge Handbook of Contemporary Thailand*, London: Routledge, 2019, pp. 36–52.

Waylen, Georgina, "Women and Democratization: Conceptualizing Gender Relations in Transition Politics," *World Politics*, Vol. 46, No. 3, April 1994, pp. 327–354.

Welzel, Christian, "Theories of Democratization," in Christian Haerpfer, Patrick Bernhagen, Christian Welzel, and Ronald F. Inglehart, eds., *Democratization*, 2nd ed., Oxford, United Kingdom: Oxford University Press, 2019, pp. 21–39.

Wickramasinghe, Nira, *Sri Lanka in the Modern Age: A History*, New York: Oxford University Press, 2014.

Wongcha-um, Panu, and Panarat Thepgumpanat, "How Thailand's Coup Leader Kept Power Through Election," Reuters, June 5, 2019. As of May 24, 2021:
https://www.reuters.com/article/us-thailand-politics-military-analysis/
how-thailands-coup-leader-kept-power-through-election-idUSKCN1T62AS

World Bank, "Open Data," database, undated a. As of October 26, 2021:
https://data.worldbank.org/

———, "World Development Indicators," database, undated b. As of November 9, 2021:
https://databank.worldbank.org/reports.aspx?source=world-development-indicators

World Integrated Trade Solution, "Sri Lanka Trade," webpage, undated. As of June 10, 2021:
https://wits.worldbank.org/countrysnapshot/en/LKA

World Inequality Database, homepage, undated. As of October 31, 2021:
https://wid.world/data/

World Trade Organization, "Regional Trade Agreements," database, undated. As of October 27, 2021:
http://rtais.wto.org/UI/PublicMaintainRTAHome.aspx